AIR FRYER COOKBOOK FOR BEGINNERS

1000 Days Simple & Quick Recipes with Inexpensive Ingredients to Improve Your Diet for Beginners and Advanced Users.
British Measurements & Ingredients

Nathan Terrell

Table of Contents

CHAPTER 1: Introduction

What Is An Air Fryer?

A kitchen equipment known as an air fryer is a device that converts air into heat in order to cook food. It circulates hot air over the food, evaporating moisture and creating a crispy outer crust. Air fryers perform best when the surrounding air is dry and above room temperature. Moist air causes food to steam and loses its crispiness and taste, resulting in bland fried food. Air frying cooks dishes quicker than traditional techniques such as baking, boiling, or roasting. Because of the crispy surface, it's a wonderful method to prepare chips, roast potatoes, and a variety of other potato side dishes without deep-frying them in oil.

The air fryer operates on the same concept as convection ovens, with hot air being discharged in one direction and rising to the top level. In this situation, heated food is put within a sealed container (usually a perforated sealed bag or tube), and hot air is pumped inside it. The heated air minimizes food contamination as it cooks. A blower fan pumps hot air into the container of the air fryer. This brings the temperature inside the meal up to 200 °C, which is enough to cook it quickly and evenly.

Air fryers vary greatly; some types do not need any preheating time. Models with a longer warm-up time may use more energy. Some air fryers have a rotisserie attachment for cooking meat and poultry, fish, and other items with a crispy outside and soft inside.

Convection cooking is used in many models, which decreases cooking time by around 30% compared to traditional ovens and reduces fat consumption by about 10%.

Cooking efficiency varies based on the size of the container and how often the contents need to be emptied. The lifespan of an air fryer varies based on the type and may be influenced by a number of things.

The most common reason for replacing an air fryer is if it malfunctions, if it has a faulty motor, or if it has worn-out components. Another possibility is that food becomes stuck and causes a mess, stopping the device from performing its duty. Just like other appliances, when used for a lengthy period of time, the heating element may begin to malfunction or deteriorate.

Your air fryer gets very hot inside, which helps to ensure that the food cooks quickly and effectively. It serves as a miniature oven, so you can think of the food as baked or roasted, but because of the additional heat, it's closer to fried food in terms of its texture. You should see a lovely golden color developing on most foods as they cook, and this is an indication that the outside is turning deliciously crispy.

Because of the ease with which air fryers may be operated, even inexperienced cooks don't have to stress when it comes to ensuring that they are preparing their food in the "proper" manner. This is one of the many advantages of using an air fryer. When you're cooking with an air fryer, all you need to do is put the food in the basket and occasionally shake it – and then wait for it to be ready. It is advisable not to walk away while your air fryer is cooking because of the high temperatures involved; if something cooks more quickly than expected and you aren't around, there's a risk of it burning.

It does also help to occasionally take the basket out and give the food a little shake to ensure that the air is able to flow evenly over all parts of it – but otherwise, it couldn't be easier! This is one of the reasons that air fryers are so popular with beginner chefs; it is possible to cook wonderful food with minimal effort, and one does not have to be an expert in order to produce something remarkable.

How Do You Use An Air Fryer?

Liable on the type of air fryer and the manufacturing company that has made it, air fryer machines can vary. Each machine will have different buttons and settings, and it will come with its own instruction manual.

However, there are some general guidelines that you can follow for almost any kind of air fryer. Below, we've listed the key steps to take when you're cooking using an air fryer. If you're unsure how to use your machine after using these steps, make sure to take a look at the instruction manual.

1. Make a decision on which of the scrumptious dishes contained in this book you would like to make, and then gather all of the essential materials.

2. You will need to start by preheating the air fryer and then lining the mesh bin of the air fryer with baking parchment or oil before beginning to follow the recipe.

3. Follow the recipe until you're ready to put the food into the air fryer basket. Transfer your ingredients very carefully into the lined mesh basket, being careful not to touch the heating elements or overfill the basket. Always be cautious when using an air fryer. The heating elements can pose a health and safety risk, so make sure to carefully transfer your ingredients in and out of the mesh basket.

4. If you want your food to be extra crispy, you can add a small coating of oil to the ingredients before or after placing them in the air fryer.

5. Shut the air fryer lid and choose the correct temperature setting. Many air fryer machines have pre-set cooking times and temperatures to choose from, or you can decide your own settings.

6. Once the lid is closed, all you need to do is wait or continue preparing the rest of your meal. When the food is cooked to your desired crispiness, carefully remove it from the mesh basket and serve.

7. Wait for the machine to cool down before cleaning the mesh basket in preparation for the next time you want to use the machine.

CHAPTER 2: Benefits Of Using an Air Fryer

Here are some of the benefits you can get out of using an air fryer:

Healthier Cooking

Everyone agrees that food cooked in an air fryer has less than half the fat of the same food cooked in a deep fat fryer, and that means far fewer calories. Great news for people with type 2 diabetes or heart conditions – although all health professionals agree that you shouldn't live just on food cooked in your air fryer. The dishes you cook should be a balanced diet that includes fresh fruit and vegetables.

Several studies have found that food cooked in an air fryer has lower levels of a substance called acrylamide. This can be a cancer-causing agent and is naturally created when starchy foods, such as potatoes, are cooked at high temperatures for a long time. So, reducing the amount of starch by soaking starchy vegetables before cooking, along with shorter cooking times and less oil, are thought to reduce levels of acrylamide.

Helps in Weight Loss

Obesity has been linked to many chronic illnesses, including hypertension. Though not initially intended to be used for weight loss, the use of an air fryer has also been proven to aid in weight loss due to the limited use of oil during cooking which allows you to avoid deep frying.

Safer and Easier

Nothing scares me more than a hot pot of oil. It is an accident waiting to happen, and getting struck with burning oil splatters is no joke! But this, and its corresponding injuries, is often the price to pay for deep-fried foods.

Air Fryers are also user-friendly, and this makes a huge difference. You don't have to feel like you are studying for a degree when working with an Air Fryer. Making dinner is far less complicated in an Air Fryer than many of the traditional methods of cooking. For some meals—you can even revert to placing a small piece of meat (even if it happens to be frozen!) into the basket and select the cooking settings.

The simplicity of the Air Fryer is its beauty. You will save countless time and unnecessary frustrations and still make delicious food!

Faster Than Cooking in the Oven

Once you buy an Air Fryer and set it to heat for the first time, you won't know what hit you! The average normal oven needs about 10 minutes to preheat. Due to the Air Fryer's smaller size and innovative design, it will be ready to go in no time!

It's even faster during the actual cooking. With the circulation that allows your food to be cooked crisp and even, it cuts a whole lot of cooking time out of the equation. This is amazing, especially in this day and age where technology, work, friends, family, and even pets are constantly demanding our attention.

Just imagine! You could set your food in the Air Fryer, and (with some recipes) it will be ready to eat in less than 20 minutes!

Saves Space

An Air Fryer is perfect for you if you live in a small apartment or student accommodation. Air Fryers are much smaller in comparison to a conventional oven, and you can easily make use of this Air Fryer in 1 cubic foot of your kitchen.

You can even pack your Air Fryer away after use if need be, but the majority of people choose to keep it out on the counter. But it's nice to have the option to move your Air Fryer around if space becomes an issue.

Low Operating Costs

Considering how much cooking oil costs these days and the amount you need to use, you will soon be cutting costs in making deep fried foods. All an Air Fryer uses is a small amount of oil and some of the electricity to power up the Air Fryer, about the same amount that a countertop oven would.

Not only will you be cutting out the massive oil costs, which will save money, you will likely also save money by ordering out less, as you'll be able to replicate your favorite foods quickly and easily at home!

No Oil Smell

In reality, it's not cool to smell like that of the meal you just ate, no matter how good the food was. But this is usually what happens when people eat deep-fried foods.

When deep frying foods, it also causes the whole house to smell, and as the oil splatters around, it can leave a massive mess. The oil can even harden on the walls, causing grime to build up into a nasty concentration of dirt and grease.

With less cooking oil, Air Fryers don't have any of those oil smells and keeps the space cleaner around you, as all the oils, smells, and actual cooking are contained within the machine.

Preserves Nutrients

When you are cooking your food in an Air Fryer, it actually protects the food from losing all its moisture. This means that using a little oil and the circulation of hot air can allow your food to keep most of its nutrients, which is excellent for you!

If you want to cook healthy foods to maintain as many nutrients as possible, then an Air Fryer is perfect for you!

Easier to Clean

Cleaning is perhaps the bane of my existence, especially after cooking and having a long day. This can really take away a lot of the pleasure of making yourself a great meal. But an Air Fryer lightens the burden by being easy to clean!

Consistent cleaning after using it (much like any pot or pan) can allow for easier and simpler living. You just need some soapy water and a non-scratch sponge to clean both the exterior and the interior of your Air Fryer. Some Air Fryers are even dishwasher-safe!

Great Flavor

The flavor of Air Fryer "fried" foods is nearly identical to traditional frying, and the texture is exact. You can cook a lot of those great frozen foods, like onion rings or French fries, and still achieve that crunchy effect. This certainly can help you turn to healthier foods, especially if your goal is for healthy but quality meals.

The Air Fryer helps to cook your food to perfect crispness, instead of the soggy mess that happens when you try alternative methods of cooking foods that are meant to be deep fried (like chicken tenders). No one enjoys mushy food. The Air Fryer keeps that desired element while remaining healthy.

All you will need is just some cooking oil sprayed outside your food to end up with a cooked interior and a crunchy exterior. So, no worries! You can still eat your foods with a crunch and a healthier result!

Versatile

Unlike cookers meant just for rice or bread makers meant just for bread, you will find that an Air Fryer leaves a lot of room to be both versatile and healthier. You can cook almost anything you would like in the Air Fryer (as long as it fits). From spaghetti squash to desserts, even to fried chicken!

You will probably never run out of air frying options!

CHAPTER 3: Air Fryer Tips And Tricks

If you're concerned about your health, you may want to consider an air fryer as a healthier option for deep-frying. While it does take up space, it is well worth the expenditure since it is simple to clean and requires minimal oil.

1. **Don't fill the basket all the way:** If you're making a snack with many bits, fill it halfway instead of filling it all the way. This enables the oil to flow more freely and ensures that everything cooks evenly. You may always add additional pieces to the basket if it isn't full enough.

2. **Do not allow the oil to get too hot:** Hot oil will not circulate effectively. It will collect at the bottom and cover everything as it makes its way to the basket. As a result, make sure the oil isn't overly hot, which may happen rapidly if you're preparing a significant quantity of food. By adding a few droplets of oil to the basket, you can see how hot it is. If it sizzles and bubbles, lower the heat by turning it down or adding additional cold water.

3. **Use the proper temperature and time:** There are several kinds of air fryers, and the majority of them cook at varying temperatures. Before you begin cooking, read the directions for each one if you are unfamiliar with them. The temperature you should use depends on what you're cooking. If you're cooking anything with a lot of liquid, like chicken wings, use a lower temperature to keep the oil from popping or boiling.

4. **Use a thermometer:** A thermometer ensures that your food is properly and completely cooked. If you don't have one, most air fryers feature built-in thermometers that you may use to adjust the temperature and time before leaving it to cook. Check that the temperature is not higher than advised and that the gadget beeps when the dish is ready to serve.

5. **Cook in small batches:** You might want to cook a lot of food at once, but doing so will stop the oil from moving around well enough. Every other item of food you add will cling to the bottom of the basket, making it more difficult for them to cook correctly. Instead, make small amounts to achieve the greatest possible outcome for your cuisine.

6. **Use precision cooking:** Precision cooking ensures that whatever you make turns out well every time. This enables you to set the temperature on a timer, giving you complete control over your food and guaranteeing optimal cooking. This setting is ideal for preparing meals and cleaning the air fryer before going to bed. If your food is still cooking after the timer runs out, you may reset it, and your air fryer will remember the temperature you set it at.

7. **Use a non-stick pan or mat:** In order to avoid food from becoming stuck to the base of the basket or pan, you will need to use a pan that is non-stick. It also helps in cleaning if any particles get caught in your pan. It takes a lot of skill to use the non-stick mat correctly, so you aren't constantly wiping it up, but it's worth the work. If you don't have any, you may use parchment paper or bits of foil to keep your basket from sticking too much to the bottom.

8. **Check the basket regularly:** When cooking most items, you should check it frequently. To prevent overcooking and dryness while cooking anything that you want to become crispy, flip the meal halfway through cooking. Check your items to determine whether they need more of a certain component, such as chicken wings or asparagus, which may require more oil than what is currently

in the basket. You may even shake and swirl the basket while it's cooking to make sure the food cooks evenly.

9. **Clean before each use:** To prevent build up after cooking, always clean your air fryer before each use. Some models even feature detachable baskets that may be simply cleaned after you're finished. You may also clean the basket with a sponge after soaking it in diluted bleach. Some air fryers even come with brushes intended to help clean the basket easier since food gets trapped in it and may not come out easily.

10. **Choose healthy oil:** You'll want to use healthy oil for your air fryer since it's not beneficial if your food goes rancid after heating. You may also find various oils to use, and even air fryers come with built-in oils, so you don't have to buy them separately.

CHAPTER 4: How To Clean An Air Fryer?

Cleaning the air fryer after frying chicken, fries, or baking pizza is necessary. A thorough cleaning helps the appliance get rid of the grease and makes maintenance of the device easier. Let us guide you on how to clean your air fryer.

Things you will need:

- Baking soda
- Microfiber cloths or cotton
- Non-abrasive sponge
- A toothbrush or soft-bristled brush
- Dish soap

Turn off and unplug your air fryer:

Switch off the equipment and unplug it. Leave the air fryer until it cools down. It may take half an hour to cool or quicker if you remove its basket or pan from the machine.

Wipe the machine

Use a damp microfiber cloth or cotton to wipe the outside of the machine. Once done, dip the non-abrasive sponge in hot water to clean the inside of the device.

Remove the food particles

If any hard-stuck food particle does not come off from the surface or body of the appliance, make a paste of baking soda using water and rub the dirty spots with a soft brush or non-abrasive sponge. Wipe it using a microfiber cloth or cotton.

Wash the pan and the basket

Many air fryer companies claim their appliances to be dishwasher safe. You need to place them in the dishwasher and run your regular cycle. If your air fryer is not dishwasher-safe, cleaning the pan and the basket is easy and does not take much time. Use warm and mild detergent to wash the fryer and dry it with a lint-free soft towel.

Soak the pan and the basket

If harsh food particles are stuck on the pan or basket, soak them in hot water for ten minutes. Using a non-abrasive sponge, clean the surfaces to remove the hard-stuck residue. Repeat until your appliance is free from the entire residue.

Dry all the parts

Before reassembling your appliance, ensure all the parts are dry, and there are no water droplets inside the machine. Drying the pan, basket, and central unit is essential, especially before reassembling them.

Air Fryers Safety Tips

Even though you won't be using large amounts of oil in your air fryer, monitoring the device while it is in use is still important. Don't assume that you can leave the air fryer for long periods of time. While the cooking time will be significantly reduced, you should actively check your food throughout the cooking process.

A few safety tips to keep in mind while cooking with your air fryer:

- Check your food often. No one wants to eat a burned dinner. But burning food can present not just a bad meal but also a dangerous situation. Be sure to check your meal several times while cooking.

- Keep your air fryer unplugged when not in use. It's always a good idea to keep any appliance unplugged when you aren't using it. This habit prevents the device from unintentionally being activated.

- Operate your air fryer away from water. Of course, since your air fryer is electrically operated, you'll want to ensure you are not using it near any large amounts of water, especially while plugged in. Doing so can result in shock or electrocution. You'll want to be mindful of sink water and pitchers or glasses of water nearby while you're cooking.

- Clean your air fryer frequently. Keep your device free of crumbs, oil, and other build up. Allowing debris to build up over time can result in a fire hazard. Be sure to wash the basket and any trays according to instructions.

- Use the appropriate tools. Be sure you are using only approved accessories for your air fryer's particular make and model. Not using the right-shaped accessories or ones not intended for your device can lead to melted materials and improperly cooked foods.

- Read the instruction manual. Don't be tempted to just "wing" using an air fryer for the first few times. Read the manual that came with your fryer thoroughly before using. Save the manual in an easy-to-reach place so that you can consult it as necessary throughout your time in the kitchen.

CHAPTER 5: Breakfast

Cinnamon French Toast

Preparation time: 10 minutes

Cooking time: 5 minutes

Servings: 2

Ingredients:

- 4 slices bread
- 4 eggs
- 200 ml milk
- 30 g brown sugar
- 5 g ground cinnamon
- 15 g honey

Directions:

1. Put your air fryer through its paces by preheating it to 150 degrees Celsius and lining the lower part of the basket using cookie sheet.
2. Divide all slices of bread into 2 even rectangles.
3. Whisk the 4 eggs, milk, brown sugar, as well as grounded cinnamon inside a stirring container.
4. Soak the bread slices in the egg mixture 'til they are fully covered.
5. After the bread has been soaked, place it in the air fryer chambers that have been lined with parchment paper, shut the cover, and let the bread bake for five mins.
6. Serve the French toast slices using a drizzle of cinnamon as well as a sprinkle of extra cinnamon.

Per serving: Calories: 256kcal; Fat: 5g; Protein: 5g; Carbs: 16g

Breakfast Toasties

Preparation time: 10 minutes

Cooking time: 5 minutes

Servings: 1

Ingredients:

- 2 slices bread
- 5 ml tomato sauce
- 1 fried egg
- 2 sausages, cooked
- 1 hash brown, cooked

Directions:

1. The air fryer should be preheated to 150 degrees Celsius, and the lower part of the bucket should be lined using cookie sheet.
2. Lay one slice of bread on a clean surface and spread 5g of tomato sauce evenly across the top. Lay the fried egg on top.
3. After slicing the sausages in 1/2 lengthwise, set these on top of the egg, then place the hash brown on top of the sausages.
4. Bring the second slice of bread on top and gently press down to seal the ingredients into the sandwich.
5. Bake the bread inside the air fryer for five mins after transferring it there. After two mins of cooking on one side, flip the toasted sandwich and continue cooking it on the opposite end for a total of four mins.

Per serving: Calories: 278kcals; Fat: 10g; Protein: 12g; Carbs: 25g

BBQ Chicken Toasted Wraps

Preparation time: 15 minutes

Cooking time: 10 minutes

Servings: 4

Ingredients:

- 100 g cooked chicken breast slices
- 60 ml BBQ sauce
- 4 whole meal wraps
- 60 g cheddar cheese, grated

Directions:

1. The air fryer should be preheated to 180 degrees Celsius, and the lower part of the bucket should be lined with cookie sheet.
2. Put the pieces of chicken breast in a tiny stirring container, and then pour the barbecue sauce over them. Toss the chicken throughout the sauce so that it is completely covered.
3. Lay the whole meal wraps out on a clean surface and evenly spread the BBQ chicken breast chunks in the center of each one.
4. Add 15 g of cheddar cheese on top of the chicken chunks.
5. Fold the left and right sides of each wrap over to cover the filling, followed by the top and bottom to form a square.
6. Put the wrapped contents into the air fryer once you have secured the covering with a cocktail straw around the components. Heat the packaging for eight to ten mins, or till it has a toasted brown colour and is crunchy.

Per serving: Calories: 256kcal; Fat: 6g; Protein: 12g; Carbs: 18g

Air Fryer Garlic Bread

Preparation time: 5 minutes

Cooking time: 5 minutes

Servings: 4

Ingredients:

- 60 g butter, softened
- 2 garlic cloves, peeled and minced
- 5 g dried chives
- 4 large ciabatta breads
- 30 g Parmesan cheese, grated

Directions:

1. The air fryer should be preheated to 180 degrees Celsius, and the lower part of the bucket should be lined with cookie sheet.
2. Combine the butter, minced garlic cloves, and dried chives in a small mixing bowl.
3. Lay the 4 ciabatta rolls on a clean surface and spread the garlic butter mixture evenly across one side. Top each slice with 15 g grated Parmesan cheese.
4. The ciabatta pieces should now be placed in the air fryer. Heat for another five mins, or till the cheese has dissolved on base as well as the ciabatta has turned golden brown and crunchy.

Per serving: Calories: 117kcal; Fat: 8g; Protein: 3g; Carbs: 12g

Egg Fried Rice

Preparation time: 5 minutes

Cooking time: 15 minutes

Servings: 4

Ingredients:

- 400 g cooked white rice
- 15 ml olive oil
- 2 eggs, scrambled

Directions:

1. The air fryer should be preheated to 180 degrees Celsius, and the lower part of the bucket should be lined with cookie sheet.
2. Inside a container, mix cooked rice and olive oil. Toss to coat before folding in the scrambled egg.
3. Transfer the rice to the prepared air fryer basket and fry for fifteen mins. Offer using some curry, chili, or mixed vegetables.

Per serving: Calories: 213kcal; Fat: 6g; Protein: 9g; Carbs: 18g

Vegetable Rice

Preparation time: 5 minutes

Cooking time: 15 minutes

Servings: 4

Ingredients:

- 400 g cooked white or brown rice
- 100 g frozen mixed vegetables
- 15 ml olive oil

Directions:

1. The air fryer should be preheated to 180 degrees Celsius, and the lower part of the bucket should be lined with cookie sheet.
2. Put the cooked rice inside a container then stir in the frozen mixed vegetables.
3. Include 15 ml olive oil, then toss to fully coat the rice. Transfer to the air fryer basket, then cook for 15 minutes until the rice has softened.
4. Serve as an accompaniment to your main course for supper, or prepare a rice bowl and top it with sliced chicken or tofu for lunch.

Per serving: Calories: 198kcal; Fat: 4g; Protein: 8g; Carbs: 14g

Air Fryer Naan Bread Pizzas

Preparation time: 5 minutes

Cooking time: 5 minutes

Servings: 2

Ingredients:

- 2 plain naan bread
- 30 g tomato paste
- 50 g mozzarella cheese, grated
- 5 g dried basil

Directions:

1. The air fryer should be preheated to 180 degrees Celsius, and the lower part of the bucket should be lined with cookie sheet.
2. Spread 15 g tomato paste evenly on top of each naan bread.
3. Sprinkle some grated mozzarella on top of the tomato paste and 2.5 g of dried basil on each naan.
4. After placing the naan bread pizzas inside the air fryer bucket that has been prepared, bake them for five mins, or till the cheese has dissolved and the crust is brown.
5. Serve the pizzas with a side salad for lunch or dinner.

Per serving: Calories: 214kcal; Fat: 10g; Protein: 8g; Carbs: 16g

Cinnamon Bagels

Preparation time: 10 minutes

Cooking time: 10 minutes

Servings: 4

Ingredients:

- 400 g self-rising flour
- 30 g granulated sugar
- 10 g ground cinnamon
- 120 ml Greek yogurt
- 15 ml olive oil
- 1 egg

Directions:

1. The air fryer should be preheated to 180 degrees Celsius, and the lower part of the bucket should be lined with cookie sheet.
2. Inside a big mixing container, mix the flour, granulated sugar, and cinnamon.
3. Stir in Greek yogurt and olive oil. Whisk well to combine the ingredients into a smooth and sticky dough.
4. Form the dough into eight spheres of similar size. Put some pressure on every ball with your palms to flatten them into patties.
5. Use your thumb to create holes in the center of each patty to form bagels.
6. In a bowl, whisk the eggs. Use a pastry brush to lightly coat each bagel in the beaten egg.
7. Place the bagels in an air fryer and bake for ten mins, or till they have achieved a golden colour.
8. Allow them to cool for 10 minutes. Serve with some cream cheese, butter, or peanut butter on top.

Per serving: Calories: 180kcal; Fat: 5g; Protein: 7g; Carbs: 18g

Crispy Pizza Bites

Preparation time: 5 minutes

Cooking time: 10 minutes

Servings: 4

Ingredients:

- 8 x frozen pizza bites
- 5 g dried chives
- 5 g black pepper

Directions:

1. The air fryer should be preheated to 180 degrees Celsius, and the lower part of the bucket should be lined with cookie sheet.
2. Place the pizza bites in the air fryer. Sprinkle some dried chives and black pepper over the top of each one.
3. Cook for eight to ten mins, till the temperature reaches desired levels and the cheese has dissolved.
4. Offer the pizza bites as part of a buffer or as a refreshment.

Per serving: Calories: 175kcal; Fat: 7g; Protein: 6g; Carbs: 14g

Sweet Potato Hash

Preparation time: 15 minutes

Cooking time: 26 minutes

Servings: 6

Ingredients:

- 2 sweet potatoes, cubed
- 2 slices of bacon, small cubes
- 30 ml olive oil
- 15 g smoked paprika
- 5 g salt
- 5 g black pepper (ground)
- 5 g dill weed (dried)

Directions:

1. Start by preheating the "Air Fryer" at 200 degrees Celsius.
2. Put the olive oil into a big basin and set it aside.
3. Put the potatoes, bacon, salt, pepper, dill, and paprika into the container, and swirl everything together so that it is uniformly seasoned.
4. Put the ingredients of the container into the "Air Fryer" and set the timer for twelve to sixteen mins. Stir the contents of the Air Fryer at the halfway point.
5. Serve.

Per serving: Calories: 152kcal; Fat: 6g; Protein: 3.5g; Carbs: 21.5g

Egg & Ham Cups

Preparation time: 14 minutes

Cooking time: 20 minutes

Servings: 4

Ingredients:

- 4 eggs
- 8 slices of bread, pre-toasted
- 2 slices of ham
- A pinch of salt
- A pinch of pepper
- A little extra butter for greasing

Directions:

1. Take 4 ramekins and brush them with butter to grease the inside.
2. Take the slices of bread and flatten them down with a rolling pin.
3. Arrange the toast inside the ramekins, rolling it around the sides, with 2 slices in each ramekin.

4. Line the inside of each ramekin with a slice of ham.

5. Every ramekin should have 1 egg cracked into it.

6. Add some salt, pepper, and other seasonings to taste.

7. Next, transfer the ramekins to the "Air Fryer" and set the temperature to 160 degrees Celsius. Boil for fifteen mins.

8. Take out of the fryer and stand in line until it has cooled down a little bit.

9. After removing from the ramekins, the dish can then be served.

Per serving: Calories: 204kcal; Fat: 6g; Protein: 12g; Carbs: 24g

Chocolate Chip Cookies

Preparation time: 10 minutes

Cooking time: 15 minutes

Ingredients:

Servings: 12

- 115 g butter, melted
- 55 g brown sugar
- 50 g caster sugar
- 1 large egg
- 5 ml pure vanilla extract
- 185 g plain flour
- 2.5 ml bicarbonate of soda
- 2.5 g salt
- 120 g chocolate chips
- 35 g chopped walnuts

Directions:

1. Take a medium bowl and whisk together melted butter and sugars.

2. Include egg and vanilla, and whisk until incorporated.

3. Add salt, flour, and bicarbonate of soda and stir.

4. Arrange a small piece of parchment in the Air Fryer's basket, ensuring air flow around the edges.

5. Work in batches, using a large cookie scoop and scoop dough onto parchment, about 45 g, leaving 5cm between each. Press to flatten slightly.

6. Bake inside the "Air Fryer" at 180 degree Celsius for eight mins. Cookies will be golden and slightly soft. Let them cool for five mins prior to offering.

Per serving: Calories: 224kcal; Fat: 13g; Protein: 3.5g; Carbs: 24g

Vegetable Frittata

Preparation time: 5 minutes

Cooking time: 10 minutes

Servings: 1

Ingredients:

- Oil or butter to grease the pan
- 3 eggs
- 1/4 red pepper, diced
- 1/4 green pepper, diced
- 10 baby spinach leaves, chopped
- A handful of cheddar cheese, grated
- Salt and pepper to season, optional

Directions:

1. Grab a container then whisk the eggs within; then, sprinkle the container using some salt and pepper.
2. Prepare the saucepan by coating this in oil or butter, then putting it into the "Air Fryer" to heat up. Change the temperature to 180 degrees Celsius, and let it warm up for one min. After adding the peppers, continue to simmer for another three mins.
3. The spinach and egg mixture should be poured in here. Cheese gratings should be sprinkled over the surface. Continue boiling for a further six mins while monitoring the temperature to make sure it doesn't burn.

Per serving: Calories: 514kcal; Fat: 31g; Protein: 38g; Carbs: 18g

Sausage Sandwiches

Preparation time: 11 minutes

Cooking time: 15 minutes

Servings: 4

Ingredients:

- 4 breakfast sausage patties
- 4 eggs
- Kosher salt, pepper
- 15 g butter
- 4 bagel thins or English muffins
- 4 slices of cheese of choice

Directions:

1. Place the bacon meatballs for breakfast into the bucket of the "air fryer". Prepare the "Air Fryer" to cook at 200 degrees Celsius for fifteen mins.
2. Take the sausage out of the pan and place it on a few toilet papers so that the extra fat can dry out.
3. Pick up a container and give the eggs a good beating within it. Inside a pan of mid-sized, season with salt and pepper, then melt butter over a flame setting of moderate-low. After it has dissolved, include the eggs that have been whisked inside an uniform sheet.

4. Fry for two to three mins before flipping. Continue to fry for 1 to 2 mins. Take the eggs out of the saucepan and then slice them into four evenly sized.

5. Place the lower half of the English toast or bagel inside the bowl of the "Air Fryer". After that, place sausage patties on upper side of every, followed by a cut of cheese as well as an egg that has been fried.

6. Over the top of every sandwich, place the toasted upper part of the English muffin or the bagel.

7. For four to five mins, adjust the "Air Fryer" to a temperature of 200 degrees Celsius.

8. Serve.

Per serving: Calories: 323kcal; Fat: 13g; Protein: 22g; Carbs: 29g

Cheese Omelette

Preparation time: 10 minutes

Cooking time: 10 minutes

Servings: 1

Ingredients:

- 2 eggs
- 150 ml milk
- Pinch of salt
- 40g shredded cheese
- Any toppings you like, such as mushrooms, peppers, onions, etc

Directions:

1. Inside a medium mixing jug, mix the eggs as well as milk
2. Include the salt and garnishes and mix well
3. Take a 15x8 cm pan and grease well before pouring the mixture inside
4. Arrange the bowl inside the "Air Fryer" basket
5. Bake at 170 °C for ten mins
6. At the halfway point, sprinkle the cheese on top and loosen the edges with a spatula
7. Remove and enjoy!

Per serving: Calories: 395kcal; Fat: 27g; Protein: 25g; Carbs: 7g

French Toast Sticks

Preparation time: 5 minutes

Cooking time: 10 minutes

Servings: 6

Ingredients:

- 45 g of caster sugar
- Salt

- 80 ml of double cream
- 1.125 g of ground cinnamon
- 2.5 ml of vanilla extract
- 6 thick slices of white loaf or brioche, each slice cut into thirds
- Maple syrup, for serving
- 2 large eggs
- 80 ml of whole milk

Directions:

1. Take a large shallow baking dish and beat sugar, cream, eggs, cinnamon, vanilla, milk, and a pinch of salt.
2. After adding the bread, give it a couple turns to cover it.
3. Place the French bread in the bowl of the "Air Fryer", operating in stages as necessary to prevent the container from becoming overcrowded. Adjust the temperature of the "Air Fryer" to 190 degrees Celsius and fry the chicken for approximately eight mins, turning it over midway over.
4. To distribute, sprinkle using maple syrup while still heated.

Per serving: Calories: 166kcal; Fat: 7g; Protein: 6g; Carbs: 18g

CHAPTER 6: Meat

Beef Meatballs

Preparation time: 30 minutes

Cooking time: 15 minutes

Servings: 4

Ingredients:

- 100 g plain flour
- 100 g rolled oats
- 100 g whole meal crackers
- 2 eggs, beaten
- 1 pc - 400 ml can evaporated milk
- 5 g onion powder
- 5 g garlic powder
- 5 g cayenne pepper
- 5 g salt
- 800 g ground minced beef

Directions:

1. The "air fryer" should be preheated to 180 degrees Celsius, and the lower part of the bucket should be lined using cookie sheet.
2. Inside a big mixing container, combine the plain flour, rolled oats, and whole meal crackers. Stir in the beaten eggs and evaporated milk and stir thoroughly.
3. Put some salt, onion powder, garlic powder, as well as cayenne pepper in a container then mix them all together.
4. After incorporating the meat in the combination, give it a good swirl to ensure that everything is well combined.
5. Use a spoon to gather small amounts of the mixture. Roll into equal balls.
6. After you have prepped the "air fryer" bucket, place the meatballs in it then fry for fifteen mins, or till they are crunchy and golden.
7. Offer the meatballs hot using spaghetti and tomato sauce.

Per serving: Calories: 248kcal; Fat: 12g; Protein: 21g; Carbs: 14g

Air Fryer Pigs in Blankets

Preparation time: 10 minutes

Cooking time: 10 minutes

Servings: 4

Ingredients:

- 16 cocktail sausages
- 8 strips streaky bacon
- 15 ml olive oil

Directions:

1. The "air fryer" should be preheated to 180 degrees Celsius, and the lower part of the bucket should be lined using cookie sheet.
2. Cut the bacon slices in half.
3. Wrap the 16 cocktail sausages in the streaky bacon slices.
4. Olive oil should be used to coat the sausages and pork before placing them in the "air fryer". Grill the pork for ten mins, or until it reaches the desired level of crispiness.

Per serving: Calories: 89kcal; Fat: 5g; Protein: 4g; Carbs: 5g

Roast Pork

Preparation time: 20 minutes

Cooking time: 15 minutes

Servings: 4

Ingredients:

- 1 large pork loin
- 5 g salt
- 5 g black pepper

Directions:

1. Use a razor blade to make slits in the ham tenderloin, then wipe it well using a paper towel.
2. Top the pork using salt & black pepper, then refrigerate for 20 minutes.
3. The "air fryer" should be preheated to 200 degrees Celsius, and the lower part of the bucket should be lined using cookie sheet.
4. The pork loin should be placed in the "air fryer" using the skinned end pointing upwards. Prepare in an oven at 350 degrees for fifteen mins, till golden brown and heated completely.
5. Prior to slicing the ham in thin pieces then offering it, you should give it approximately fifteen mins to chill.

Per serving: Calories: 421kcal; Fat: 11g; Protein: 23g; Carbs: 10g

Grilled Sausages

Preparation time: 5 minutes

Cooking time: 15 minutes

Servings: 1

Ingredients:

- 2 pcs - pork sausages

- 5 g smoked paprika
- 5 g black pepper

Directions:

1. The "air fryer" should be preheated to 200 degrees Celsius, and the lower part of the bucket should be lined using cookie sheet.
2. After positioning the sausages inside the "air fryer", season them with the smoky paprika and ground black pepper.
3. Fry them for twelve to fifteen mins with the cover of the "air fryer" closed till they are heated through and browned.
4. Offer the sausages as part of all-day breakfast, inside a pasta dish, or in delicious toasties.

Per serving: Calories: 212kcal; Fat: 6g; Protein: 16g; Carbs: 8g

Beef Fried Rice

Preparation time: 10 minutes

Cooking time: 15 minutes

Servings: 3

Ingredients:

- 100 g cooked rice
- 500 g beef strips, cooked
- 15 ml sesame oil
- 1 onion, diced
- 1 egg
- 10 g garlic powder
- 15 ml vegetable oil
- 100 g frozen peas
- Salt
- Pepper

Directions:

1. The "Air Fryer" should be preheated to 175 degrees Celsius.
2. Include pepper, salt, and garlic powder to the beef.
3. Cook the beef in a pan until almost done.
4. Mix the rice with peas, carrots, and vegetable oil, combining thoroughly. Include the rice combination to the beef and mix.
5. Add to the "Air Fryer" and heat for about 10 mins.
6. Add the egg then cook until the egg has completely cooked.

Per serving: Calories: 446kcal; Fat: 14g; Protein: 44g; Carbs: 31g

Herbed Steak

Preparation time: 30 minutes

Cooking time: 20 minutes

Servings: 4

Ingredients:

- 60 g butter, softened
- 2 cloves garlic, crushed
- 10 g freshly chopped parsley
- 5 g freshly chopped chives
- 5 g freshly chopped thyme
- 5 g freshly chopped rosemary
- 1 (900g) bone-in ribeye
- Salt
- Freshly ground black pepper

Directions:

1. Combine the butter and the herbs inside a separate container. Place in the middle of a sheet of shrink paper and wrap tightly into a cylinder. After you have tightened the edges by twisting them around each other, place them in the refrigerator for twenty mins.

2. On either ends of the meat, season it with salt and pepper.

3. According to the width of the meat, put it into the bucket of the "Air Fryer" and fry it at a temperature of 200 degrees Celsius for twelve to fourteen mins for moderate, rotating it midway during the cooking process.

4. Top your steak with a slice of herb butter.

Per serving: Calories: 415kcal; Fat: 22g; Protein: 51g; Carbs: 3g

Mozzarella-Stuffed Meatballs

Preparation time: 15 minutes

Cooking time: 15 minutes

Servings: 4

Ingredients:

- 450 g beef mince
- 50 g bread crumbs
- 25 g freshly grated Parmesan
- 5 g freshly chopped parsley
- 1 large egg
- 2 cloves garlic, crushed
- 5 g dried oregano

- Salt
- Freshly ground black pepper
- 85 g fresh 363, cut into 16 cubes
- Marinara, for serving

Directions:

1. Acquire a big bowl, then mix beef, parsley, bread crumbs, Parmesan, egg, garlic, and oregano. Add salt and pepper.
2. Scoop 39 g of meat and flatten it into a patty in your hand. Arrange a cube of mozzarella in the center and pinch the meat up around the cheese, and roll it into a ball. Repeat with remaining meat to make 16 total meatballs.
3. Arrange the meatballs in the Air Fryer basket, then cook at 190 °C for 12 minutes.
4. Serve with warmed marinara.

Per serving: Calories: 363kcal; Fat: 21.5g; Protein: 30.5g; Carbs: 7g

Beef Kebobs

Preparation time: 45 minutes

Cooking time: 15 minutes

Servings: 4

Ingredients:

- 500g beef, cubed
- 200g low-fat sour cream
- 30 ml soy sauce
- 1 bell pepper
- ½ onion, chopped
- 20 x 16 cm skewers

Directions:

1. Take a medium bowl and combine the sour cream and soy sauce.
2. Add the cubed beef and marinate for at least 30 minutes.
3. Cut the pepper and onion into 2.5 cm pieces.
4. Soak the skewers in warm water for about 10 minutes.
5. Place the beef, bell peppers, and onion onto the skewers, alternating between each one.
6. Cook at 200 °C for 10 minutes, flipping halfway through.

Per serving: Calories: 250kcal; Fat: 15g; Protein: 23g ; Carbs: 4g

Pork Chops

Preparation time: 10 minutes

Cooking time: 10 minutes

Servings: 4

Ingredients:

- 4 boneless pork chops
- 30 ml extra-virgin olive oil
- 50 g freshly grated Parmesan
- 5 g salt
- 5 g paprika
- 5 g garlic powder
- 5 g onion powder
- 2.5 g freshly ground black pepper

Directions:

1. First, use a few paper tissues to remove any excess moisture from the ham chops, and afterwards bathe them in oil on either ends. Put the Parmesan and the spices in a basin of moderate size & stir well. Apply the Parmesan solution on either ends of the ham chops and then set them aside.
2. Grill the ham chops inside the "Air Fryer" bucket for nine mins at 190 degrees Celsius, turning them over once midway during the cooking process.

Per serving: Calories: 306kcal; Fat: 22g; Protein: 23g; Carbs: 1.5g

Mustard Glazed Pork

Preparation time: 2 hours 10 minutes

Cooking time: 20 minutes

Servings: 4

Ingredients:

- 750 g pork tenderloin
- 15 g minced garlic
- 1.25 g salt
- Pinch of cracked black pepper
- 45 g mustard
- 45 g brown sugar
- 5 g Italian seasoning
- 5 g rosemary

Directions:

1. Cut slits into the pork and place the minced garlic into the slits.
2. Season with salt and pepper.
3. Take a stirring container and include the rest of the components, combining well.
4. Rub the mix over the pork and allow to marinate for 2 hours.
5. Place in the "Air Fryer" and fry at 200 degrees Celsius for twenty mins.

Per serving: Calories: 256kcal; Fat: 5.5g; Protein: 23g; Carbs: 8.5g

Lamb Steaks

Preparation time: 5 minutes

Cooking time: 10 minutes

Servings: 4

Ingredients:

- 4 Lamb Steaks
- 5 g Frozen Chopped Garlic
- 10 ml Extra Virgin Olive Oil
- 10 ml Lemon Juice
- 10 ml Honey
- 5 g Thyme
- Salt & Pepper
- Fresh Mint

Directions:

1. Put the lamb steaks on a cutting panel and top it using salt, pepper, and dried thyme.
2. Thinly chop 30 g of mint and load into a bowl with everything except the lamb. Mix well, then spoon over the lamb steaks.
3. Place the steaks into the fridge for an hour, and allow them to marinate.
4. Load the steaks into the Air Fryer basket, and add extra mint.
5. Air fry for 10 minutes, 180 °C.

Per serving: Calories: 274.5kcal; Fat: 19g; Protein: 21g; Carbs: 4g

Cheesy Beef Enchiladas

Preparation time: 10 minutes

Cooking time: 5 minutes

Servings: 4

Ingredients:

- 500 g minced beef
- 1 packet of taco seasoning
- 8 medium tortillas
- 150 g grated cheese
- 100 g soured cream
- 1 can of black beans
- 1 can of tomatoes, chopped
- 1 can of chilies, chopped
- 1 can of red enchilada sauce
- A handful of cilantro, chopped

Directions:

1. Take a medium frying pan, brown the beef, and add the taco seasoning, combining well
2. Add the beef, beans, tomatoes, and chilies to the tortillas, spreading equally
3. Line the Air Fryer with foil and place the tortillas inside
4. Pour your enchilada sauce over the top, sprinkle with cheese
5. Cook at 200 °C for 5 minutes
6. Remove from the Air Fryer, add toppings and serve

Per serving: Calories: 320kcal; Fat: 43g; Protein: 25g; Carbs: 25g

Simple Hamburgers

Preparation time: 5 minutes

Cooking time: 15 minutes

Servings: 4

Ingredients:

- 500 g minced beef
- Salt
- Pepper

Directions:

1. Preheat Air Fryer to 200 °C.
2. Divide minced beef into 4 equal portions and form them into burgers with your hands.
3. Top it using salt, and pepper, to your sense of taste.
4. Air fry for 10 mins.
5. Flip your burgers over, and grill for a further three mins.

Per serving: Calories: 247.5kcal; Fat: 15g; Protein: 24g; Carbs: 0g

Beef Wellington

Preparation time: 15 minutes

Cooking time: 35 minutes

Servings: 8

Ingredients:

- 1kg beef fillet (one large piece)
- Chicken pate
- 2 sheets of short crust pastry
- 1 egg, beaten
- Salt
- Pepper

Directions:

1. Season the beef with salt and pepper and wrap tightly in cling film.
2. Place the beef in the refrigerator for at least one hour.
3. Roll out the pastry and brush the edges with the beaten egg.
4. Spread the pate over the pastry, making sure it is distributed equally.
5. Take now the beef out of the refrigerator and remove the cling film.
6. Place the beef in the middle of your pastry.
7. Wrap your pastry around the meat and seal the edges with a fork.
8. Place in the Air Fryer and cook at 160 °C for 35 minutes.

Per serving: Calories: 509kcal; Fat: 28g; Protein: 34g; Carbs: 28g

CHAPTER 7: Fish and Seafood

Breaded Cod Fillets

Preparation time: 10 minutes

Cooking time: 10 minutes

Servings: 4

Ingredients:

- 4 pcs - 100 g cod fillets
- 60 g butter, melted
- 4 garlic cloves, peeled and minced
- 2.5 g salt

Directions:

1. The "air fryer" should be preheated to 180 degrees Celsius, and the lower part of the bucket should be lined using cookie sheet.
2. Lay the cod fillets out on a clean surface.
3. Mix the butter, garlic cloves, and salt. Spoon the garlic butter mixture evenly across the surface of every fillet and mildly thumb down, so the stuffing doesn't fall off when you transfer the fillets to the air fryer.
4. Put the cod in the lined "air fryer" bucket and fry for ten mins till the fish is cooked. The fillets should fall apart when you break them using a fork.
5. Serve with some lemon and dill sauce and a side of brown rice and veggies.

Per serving: Calories: 322kcal; Fat: 3g; Protein: 29g; Carbs: 9g

Air Fryer Tuna Steak

Preparation time: 5 minutes

Cooking time: 5 minutes

Servings: 1

Ingredients:

- 1 pc - 100 g tuna steak
- 5 g salt

Directions:

1. The "air fryer" should be preheated to 180 degrees Celsius, and the lower part of the bucket should be lined using cookie sheet.
2. Sprinkle the salt over the tuna steak and put it into the mesh bucket. Grill for five mins 'til the steak has darkened.
3. Serve the tuna using your preferred sauce and sides.

Per serving: Calories: 121kcal; Fat: 4g; Protein: 18g; Carbs: 3g

Simple Salmon

Preparation time: 5 minutes

Cooking time: 20-25 minutes

Servings: 4

Ingredients:

- 4 salmon filets
- 3 lemons
- 8 sprigs rosemary
- 15 ml olive oil
- Salt

Directions:

1. Cut the lemons into tiny pieces.
2. Put several lemon slices on the bottom of the Air Fryer basket.
3. Now lay 4 rosemary sprigs on the lemons.
4. Arrange one salmon filet on top of each sprig of rosemary. Sprinkle some salt on the salmon.
5. Top each salmon filet with another sprig of rosemary. Cover with more lemon slices.
6. Sprinkle with olive oil on the surface.
7. Put the fry basket in the fryer. Keep the temp. to 135 degrees Celsius. Set the clock to twenty mins.
8. Take a fork and check the salmon; if it flakes easily, it's ready. If not, it needs 5 minutes more.
9. Serve the salmon with roasted lemon slices and rosemary.

Per serving: Calories: 242kcal; Fat: 12g; Protein: 29g; Carbs: 0g

Coconut Prawns

Preparation time: 15 minutes

Cooking time: 15 minutes

Servings: 4

Ingredients:

For The Prawns:

- 450 g of large prawns, peeled, deveined, tails on
- Freshly ground black pepper
- 65 g of plain flour
- Salt
- 35 g of shredded sweetened coconut
- 2 large eggs, beaten
- 100 g of panko bread crumbs

For The Dipping Sauce:

- 15 g of Sriracha
- 15 ml of Thai sweet chili sauce
- 120 g of mayonnaise

Directions:

1. Get a shallow container, then include salt and pepper to the flour. Take another shallow bowl, and mix bread crumbs and coconut. Arrange the eggs in a third shallow bowl.
2. Dip prawns in flour, then eggs, then coconut mixture, one at a time.
3. Arrange your prawns into the Air Fryer basket, and heat to 200 °C. Bake until the prawns are well golden and cooked through, 10-12 minutes.
4. Take a small bowl, and mix Siracha, mayonnaise, and chili sauce.
5. Serve with dipping sauce.

Per serving: Calories: 283kcal; Fat: 6.5g; Protein: 29g; Carbs: 25g

Crab Cakes

Preparation time: 20 minutes

Cooking time: 15 minutes

Servings: 4

Ingredients:

For The Crab Cakes:

- Cooking spray
- Hot sauce for serving
- Lemon wedges, for serving
- 60 g of mayonnaise
- 1 egg
- 10 g of cajun seasoning
- 5 ml of lemon zest
- 2.5 g of salt
- 450 g of jumbo lump crab meat
- 120 g of Cracker crumbs (from about 20 crackers)
- 30 g of chives, finely chopped
- 10 g of Dijon mustard

For The Tartar Sauce:

- 1.25 g of Dijon mustard
- 5 g of fresh dill, finely chopped
- 60 g of mayonnaise
- 80 g dill pickle, finely chopped

- 10 g of capers, finely chopped
- 5 ml of fresh lemon juice
- 15 g of shallot, finely chopped

Directions:

1. Get a big container, then whisk together egg, mayo, chives, Dijon mustard, lemon zest, cajun seasoning, and salt. Fold in crab meat and cracker crumbs.
2. Divide your mixture to form 8 patties.
3. Heat your Air Fryer to 190 °C, and spray the basket and the tops of your cakes with some cooking spray. Arrange the cakes in a bucket in a solo coating. Cook until crisp and deep golden brown, 12-14 minutes, and flip halfway through.
4. Get a container and combine the entire tartar sauce components.
5. Serve the cakes warm with lemon wedges, hot sauce, and tartar sauce.

Per serving: Calories: 265kcal; Fat: 8g; Protein: 24.5g; Carbs: 21g

Tilapia Fillets

Preparation time: 10 minutes

Cooking time: 10 minutes

Servings: 2

Ingredients:

- 50 g almond flour
- 2 fillets of tilapia fish
- 30 g melted butter
- 5 g black pepper
- 2.5 g salt
- 60 g mayonnaise
- A handful of almonds sliced thinly

Directions:

1. Get a mixing container and add butter, almond flour, pepper, as well as salt, combining well.
2. Take the fish and spread the mayonnaise on both sides.
3. Cover the fillets in the almond flour mix.
4. Spread one side of the fish with the sliced almonds.
5. Spray your Air Fryer with a small amount of cooking spray.
6. Add the fish to the "Air Fryer" and fry at 160 °C for ten mins.

Per serving: Calories: 500kcal; Fat: 30.5g; Protein: 33g; Carbs: 25g

Fish Tacos

Preparation time: 14 minutes

Cooking time: 10 minutes

Servings: 4

Ingredients:

- 500g mahi fish, fresh
- 8 small tortillas
- 10 g Cajun seasoning
- 60 g sour cream
- 30 g mayo
- 3.75 g cayenne
- 30 ml pepper sauce
- A little salt and pepper
- 15 ml sriracha sauce
- 30 ml lime juice

Directions:

1. Cut the fish into slices and season with salt.
2. Mix the cayenne pepper and black pepper with the Cajun seasoning. Sprinkle onto fish.
3. Brush pepper sauce on both sides of the fish.
4. The "Air Fryer" is set at 180 degrees Celsius and cook for 10 mins.
5. Take a medium bowl and combine the mayonnaise, sour cream, lime juice, sriracha, and cayenne pepper.
6. Assemble the tacos then offer!

Per serving: Calories: 447kcal; Fat: 13g; Protein: 31g; Carbs: 48g

Peppery Lemon Shrimp

Preparation time: 10 minutes

Cooking time: 10 minutes

Servings: 2

Ingredients:

- 15 ml olive oil
- 350 g prepared 208, uncooked
- Juice of 1 lemon
- 5 g pepper
- 1.25 g paprika
- 1.25 g garlic powder
- 1 lemon, sliced

Directions:

1. The "Air Fryer" should be preheated to 200 degrees Celsius.

2. Take a moderate sized mixing bowl, and combine the pepper, lemon juice, garlic powder, paprika, and olive oil together.

3. Add the shrimp to the bowl and make sure they're well coated.

4. Arrange the shrimp into the basket of the fryer

5. Cook for between 6-8 mins, till steady and pink

6. Serve!

Per serving: Calories: 208kcal; Fat: 7g; Protein: 35g; Carbs: 0g

Tuna Patties

Preparation time: 15 minutes

Cooking time: 10 minutes

Servings: 10

Ingredients:

- 425 g canned albacore tuna, drained or 454 g fresh tuna, diced
- 2-3 large eggs
- Zest of 1 medium lemon
- 15 ml lemon juice
- 1.125 g of Kosher salt, or to taste
- 55 g of bread crumbs
- 2.5 g dried herbs (oregano, dill, basil, thyme or any combo)
- Fresh cracked black pepper
- 45 g grated parmesan cheese
- 1 stalk celery, finely chopped
- Optional: tarter sauce, ranch, mayo, lemon slices
- 45 g minced onion
- 2.5 g garlic powder

Directions:

1. Get a moderate container, then combine lemon zest, eggs, lemon juice, bread crumbs, celery, parmesan cheese, onion, dried herbs, garlic powder, salt, and pepper. Now stir well. Gently fold in the tuna.

2. Take your Air Fryer perforated baking paper, then lay it inside the base of the "Air Fryer". Now lightly spray the paper. If not, you don't have it spray at the lower part of the "Air Fryer" basket to ensure they do not stick.

3. Try to keep all patties the same size and thickness. Scoop 32 g of the mixture, shape into patties about 8 cm wide x 1.3 cm thick, and lay them inside the basket. Make about 10 patties.

4. If patties are too soft, chill them for 1 hour or until firm. Brush the top of the patties with oil. Air Fry 185 °C, 10 minutes, flipping halfway through. After you flip the patties, spray the tops again.

5. Serve with your sauce and lemon slices.

Per serving: Calories: 102.2kcal; Fat: 3.9g; Protein: 12.5g; Carbs: 2.7g

Fried Cod

Preparation time: 15 minutes

Cooking time: 15 minutes

Servings: 3

Ingredients:

- 1 (450g) cod, cut into 4 strips
- Salt
- Freshly ground black pepper
- 65 g plain flour
- 1 large egg, beaten
- 200 g panko bread crumbs
- 5 g Old Bay seasoning
- Lemon wedges, for serving
- Tartar sauce, for serving

Directions:

1. Pat the fish dry and add salt and pepper on both sides.
2. Arrange egg, flour, then panko in 3 narrow containers. Include Old Bay to panko and swirl. Coat fish in the flour and in the egg, then ultimately into panko, press to coat, one at a time.
3. Arrange the fish in the "Air Fryer" basket, fry for ten to twelve mins, 200 °C, or till the fish is golden and flakes easily with a fork, gently flip halfway through.
4. Offer using lemon wedges and tartar sauce.

Per serving: Calories: 397kcal; Fat: 4.5g; Protein: 37g; Carbs: 48g

Sriracha With Salmon

Preparation time: 35 minutes

Cooking time: 15 minutes

Servings: 2

Ingredients:

- 45 g sriracha
- 60 ml honey
- 15 ml soy sauce
- 500 g salmon fillets

Directions:

1. Take a medium bowl and add the honey, soy sauce, and sriracha, combining well
2. Place the salmon into the sauce skin, with the skin facing upwards

3. Allow to marinade for 30 minutes
4. Spray the basket with some cooking spray.
5. Heat the Air Fryer to 200 °C
6. Place the salmon into the Air Fryer skin side down, then cook for 12 minutes
7. Serve!

Per serving: Calories: 505kcal; Fat: 15g; Protein: 50g; Carbs: 38.5g

Baked Crunchy Cod

Preparation time: 10 minutes

Cooking time: 15 minutes

Servings: 2

Ingredients:

- 2 pieces of cod cut into smaller portions (around five)
- 60 g of panko breadcrumbs
- 1 egg
- 1 egg white
- 2.5 g onion powder
- 2.5 g garlic salt
- A pinch of pepper
- 2.5 g mixed herbs

Directions:

1. Heat Air Fryer to 220 °C.
2. Take a small bowl and mix the egg and then add the egg white and combine once more.
3. Cover the top of the fish with the herb mixture.
4. Dip each piece of fish into the egg and then cover in the panko breadcrumbs.
5. Line Air Fryer basket with tin foil.
6. Place the fish in Air Fryer and cook for about 15 minutes.

Per serving: Calories: 291kcal; Fat: 4g; Protein: 45g; Carbs: 12g

Herby Breaded Fish

Preparation time: 12 minutes

Cooking time: 15 minutes

Servings: 4

Ingredients:

- 4 pcs – 100 g cod fillets
- 220 g breadcrumbs
- 15 g dried mixed herbs

- 50 ml oil

Directions:

1. The "Air Fryer" should be preheated to 175 degrees.
2. Combine the breadcrumbs, herbs, as well as oil inside a container.
3. Beat the egg.
4. After being dipped within the scrambled egg, every fish fillet should be coated inside the breadcrumbs mix.
5. Spray fillets with the oil and fry for twelve mins rotating the fish midway concluded.
6. Lift the fillets from the "Air Fryer" and lay them on a kitchen towel to soak up any excess fat.
7. Serve with creamy tartare sauce and potato fries or with a wedge of lemon and roasted vegetables.

Per serving: Calories: 150kcal; Fat: 3g; Protein: 10g; Carbs: 6g

CHAPTER 8: Chicken and Poultry

Chicken Wings

Preparation time: 10 minutes

Cooking time: 20 minutes

Servings: 4

Ingredients:

- 400 g chicken wings
- 5 g salt
- 5 g black pepper
- 60 ml hot sauce
- 60 ml olive oil
- 15 ml soy sauce
- 5 g garlic powder
- 5 g onion powder

Directions:

1. The "air fryer" should be preheated to 200 degrees Celsius, and the lower part of the bucket should be lined using cookie sheet.
2. Salt and pepper the chicken wings before cooking. After placing wings in the "air fryer", the cooking time should be increased to fifteen mins.
3. In the time that it takes the chicken to grill in the "air fryer", you may prepare the marinade by combining hot sauce, olive oil, soy sauce, garlic powder, and onion powder inside a container. Mixing it thoroughly requires a good whisking.
4. Take the chicken wings out of the "air fryer" and cover them inside the hot sauce using a tossing motion. After transferring to the "air fryer", continue cooking for a further five mins, or till the sauce has reached the desired consistency of being heated and viscous.
5. Serve the wings while still piping hot with a side of potato wedges and a salad.

Per serving: Calories: 99kcal; Fat: 6g; Protein: 2g; Carbs: 6g

Chicken Satay

Preparation time: 20 minutes

Cooking time: 10 minutes

Servings: 4

Ingredients:

- 400 g skinless, boneless chicken breast, cubed
- 30 ml soy sauce

- 30 ml fish sauce
- 30 ml hot sauce
- 15 g brown sugar
- 5 g garlic powder
- 10 g ground cumin
- 50 g roasted peanuts, chopped

Directions:

1. The "air fryer" should be preheated to 200 degrees Celsius, and the lower part of the bucket should be lined using cookie sheet.
2. Slices of chicken should be placed inside a container. In a separate container, thoroughly mix the soy sauce, fish sauce, spicy sauce, brown sugar, garlic powder, and powdered cumin by whisking all of the ingredients altogether till they are a homogenous mixture.
3. After pouring the sauce throughout the chicken, twist it to ensure that it is evenly coated. Allow the ingredients to marinade for twenty mins.
4. Place the chicken pieces that have been seasoned in the "air fryer" and fry for ten to twelve mins, or till they are mildly browned and crunchy.
5. Offer the chicken satay with some noodles and stir-fried vegetables topped with roasted peanuts.

Per serving: Calories: 201kcal; Fat: 8g; Protein: 18g; Carbs: 5g

Turkey Burgers

Preparation time: 10 minutes

Cooking time: 15 minutes

Servings: 4

Ingredients:

- 400 g ground turkey
- 5 g chili powder
- 5 g ground cumin
- 5 g garlic powder
- 5 g onion powder
- 15 g dried oregano
- 5 g black pepper
- 1 egg, beaten
- 15 ml sweet chili sauce

Directions:

1. The "air fryer" should be preheated to 200 degrees Celsius, and the lower part of the bucket should be lined using cookie sheet.
2. Mix the ground turkey, chili powder, ground cumin, garlic powder, onion powder, dried oregano & black pepper in a bowl.

3. Stir in the beaten egg and sweet chili sauce until all ingredients are fully combined.

4. Form the combination into four even burgers then cook in the air fryer for 18-20 mins, turning halfway through, until the meat has browned.

5. Serve the burgers in a burger bun with some fresh lettuce, tomatoes, sliced onion, and an extra squirt of sweet chili sauce.

Per serving: Calories: 298kcal; Fat: 9g; Protein: 22g; Carbs: 19g

Chicken Bites

Preparation time: 15 minutes

Cooking time: 15 minutes

Servings: 4

Ingredients:

- 3 pcs - 100 g skinless, boneless chicken breast fillets
- 2 eggs, beaten
- 15 g smoked paprika
- 5 g garlic powder
- 5 g black pepper
- 100 g breadcrumbs

Directions:

1. The "air fryer" should be preheated to 200 degrees Celsius, and the lower part of the bucket should be lined using cookie sheet.

2. Cut the chicken breasts into small chunks.

3. Mix the eggs, smoked paprika, garlic powder, and black pepper inside a stirring container.

4. Inside a distinct container, place breadcrumbs.

5. Dip the chicken chunks into the egg mixture, followed by the breadcrumbs. Toss to fully coat the chunks in breadcrumbs and transfer them into the lined air fryer basket.

6. Fry for twelve to fifteen mins until crispy and golden.

7. Serve with a side of chips or veggies.

Per serving: Calories: 278kcal; Fat: 7g; Protein: 18g; Carbs: 10g

Air Fryer Turkey Breast

Preparation time: 5 minutes

Cooking time: 10 minutes

Servings: 1

Ingredients:

- 1 pc - 100 g turkey breast steak
- 5 ml olive oil
- 5 g salt

Directions:

1. The "air fryer" should be preheated to 180 degrees Celsius, and the lower part of the bucket should be lined using cookie sheet.

2. Coat the turkey breast steak using a slight layer of olive oil. Add a little salt to the top of the steak and transfer to the air fryer. Cook for 10-12 minutes until the turkey is fully cooked and slightly golden.

3. Eat the turkey with a side of potatoes or chop it up and add it to your salads.

Per serving: Calories: 134kcal; Fat: 3g; Protein: 16g; Carbs: 4g

Tomato and Herb Chicken Breast

Preparation time: 10 minutes

Cooking time: 15 minutes

Servings: 1

Ingredients:

- 1 pc - 100 g chicken breast fillet
- 15 g tomato paste
- 5 g dried mixed herbs

Directions:

1. The "air fryer" should be preheated to 180 degrees Celsius, and the lower part of the bucket should be lined using cookie sheet.

2. Coat the chicken breast fillet with tomato paste on both sides and add a sprinkle of dried mixed herbs. Transfer to the air fryer, then cook for 12-15 minutes, turning halfway through, until golden and crispy.

3. Eat the chicken breast with a side of potatoes and vegetables.

Per serving: Calories: 145kcal; Fat: 3g; Protein: 18g; Carbs: 5g

Chicken Wings With Honey And Sesame

Preparation time: 30 mins

Cooking time: 10-30 minutes

Servings: 1–2

Ingredients:

- 450–500 g chicken wings with tips removed
- 15 ml olive oil
- 45 g corn flour
- 15 ml runny honey
- 5 ml soy sauce or tamari
- 5 ml rice wine vinegar
- 5 ml toasted sesame oil

- 10 g sesame seeds, toasted
- 1 large spring onion, thinly sliced
- Salt and freshly ground black pepper

Directions:

1. Whisk chicken wings, olive oil, as well as a sufficient quantity of salt and black pepper inside a big container. Use the bucket to hold the entire ingredients.

2. Make sure that the wings are evenly covered, swirl them inside the corn flour fifteen grams at a period until the process is complete.

3. Sauté the chicken wings in the air in single sheet for twenty-five mins at a temperature of 180 degrees Celsius, flipping them midway during the cooking process.

4. During the meantime, prepare the coating by combining the soy sauce, honey, rice, wine vinegar, as well as toasted sesame oil inside a big basin and mixing the ingredients thoroughly.

5. Next, pour the sauce over the fried wings and shake them till they are evenly covered. After additional five mins, arrange these inside a thin sheet inside the "Air Fryer" and cook them there.

6. Swirl the wings inside the sauce that is left over from the glazing. Finally, finish by topping the dish using roasted sesame seeds and chopped spring onion.

7. Offer once prepared.

Per serving: Calories: 544kcal; Fat: 32.5g; Protein: 37.5g; Carbs: 23.5g

Chicken Tenders

Preparation time: 10 minutes

Cooking time: 20 minutes

Servings: 4

Ingredients:

For The Chicken Tenders:

- 675 g chicken tenders
- Salt
- Freshly ground black pepper
- 195 g plain flour
- 250 g panko bread crumbs
- 2 large eggs
- 60 ml buttermilk
- Cooking spray

For The Honey Mustard:

- 80 g mayonnaise
- 45 g honey
- 30 g dijon mustard
- 1.25 ml hot sauce (optional)

- Pinch of salt
- Freshly ground black pepper

Directions:

1. Salt and black pepper should be applied to either ends of the chicken pieces before cooking. Put the flour and bread bits in 2 different containers that are on the smaller side. Whisk eggs and buttermilk in a third bowl. Dip chicken in flour, one at a time, then a mixture of egg and bread crumbs, pressing to season.

2. Put the chicken tenders inside your "Air Fryer" bucket, do not overcrowd it. Fry for five mins at a temperature of 200 degrees Celsius after spraying the top of the surface with cooking spray. Grill for an additional five mins after turning the chicken around and spraying the upper part using additional cooking spray. Proceed using the rest of the chicken strips in the same manner.

3. To prepare the sauce, place the honey, mayonnaise, dijon mustard, then spicy sauce in a tiny container and stir until combined. Include some coarsely ground black pepper as well as a pinch of salt.

4. Serve with honey mustard.

Per serving: Calories: 720kcal; Fat: 21g; Protein: 55g; Carbs: 74g

Rotisserie Chicken

Preparation time: 10 minutes

Cooking time: 40 minutes

Servings: 6

Ingredients:

- 10 g of onion powder
- 5 g of smoked paprika
- 1.125 g of cayenne
- 1 (1.3kg.) chicken into 8 pieces
- 10 g of dried oregano
- Salt
- 10 g of garlic powder
- Freshly ground black pepper
- 15 g of dried thyme

Directions:

1. Salt and pepper should be applied to every piece of chicken. First, combine the herbs and spices in a container of moderate size using a mixer, and afterwards massage the mixture onto the chicken.

2. Place slices of darkish meat inside the bucket of the "Air Fryer" and set the temperature to 180 degrees Celsius. Fry for ten mins, immediately turn the slices and continue cooking for another ten mins. Continue the process using the chicken breasts, however lower the cooking time to sixteen mins total, though eight mins spent on each end. Test that the chicken is roasted all the way

thoroughly by utilizing a beef thermometer; the internal temperature of every portion will read 73 degrees Celsius.

Per serving: Calories: 200kcal; Fat: 5g; Protein: 35.5g; Carbs: 0g

Chicken Nuggets

Preparation time: 20 minutes

Cooking time: 10 minutes

Servings: 4

Ingredients:

- 500 g chicken tenders
- 60 g salad dressing mix
- 30 g plain flour
- 1 egg, beaten
- 50g dry 291.5

Directions:

1. Take a huge mixing bowl, then add the chicken.
2. Sprinkle the seasoning over the top and ensure the chicken is evenly coated.
3. Allow the chicken to rest for 10 mins.
4. Add the flour into a resealable bag.
5. Pour the breadcrumbs onto a medium-sized plate.
6. Transfer the chicken into the resealable bag and coat it with the flour, giving it a good shake.
7. Remove the chicken and dip it into the egg, and then roll it into the breadcrumbs, coating evenly.
8. Repeat with the chicken.
9. Heat your Air Fryer to 200 °C.
10. Arrange the chicken inside the fryer then roast for four mins prior to turning it over and roasting for a further four mins.
11. Remove and offer whilst hot.

Per serving: Calories: 291.5kcal; Fat: 13g; Protein: 29g; Carbs: 11g

Chicken Strips

Preparation time: 30 minutes

Cooking time: 10-30 minutes

Servings: 3

Ingredients:

- 2 large garlic cloves, minced or crushed
- 75 ml plain yogurt
- 1.25 g salt, plus extra for seasoning

- 2 chicken breasts
- 90 g plain flour
- 90 g panko breadcrumbs
- 5 g sweet smoked paprika
- 5 g garlic granules
- 2.5 g cayenne pepper
- Freshly ground black pepper
- 1 free-range egg
- Olive oil cooking spray

For the creamy honey mustard dip:

- 15 ml runny honey
- 15 g light mayonnaise
- 15 g Dijon mustard
- 7.5 g wholegrain mustard
- 2.5 ml white wine vinegar

Directions:

1. Garlic, yoghurt, and salt should be mixed together and used as a marinade for the chicken. Soak the chicken inside the yoghurt mix for at least twenty mins before cutting it in pieces that are three centimeters thick.

2. To make the skimming combination, place the flour, paprika, breadcrumbs, cayenne pepper, garlic granules, as well as a sufficient quantity of salt and pepper inside a container of mid sized. Combine everything thoroughly. In a separate, smaller container, whisk the egg, then season it with salt and pepper.

3. Remove all extra yoghurt from every one of the pieces of chicken and afterwards dredge them inside the skimming combination prior to immersing them initially in the egg and afterwards into the dredged solution. Always employ a distinct set of hands when working with dry and moist substances.

4. Coat the lower part of the "Air Fryer" bucket using olive oil spray, and then spread chicken slices inside a thin sheet across the lower part of the bucket. Prior to "air-frying" the pieces for fifteen mins at 200 degrees Celsius, spray the tops of them using oil and flip them midway along the cooking process. Continue in this manner till each of the pieces are fried.

5. In the meantime, prepare the creamy honey mustard spread by combining every one of the necessary components inside a shallow dish and setting it apart.

6. Serve.

Per serving: Calories: 452kcal; Fat: 15.5g; Protein: 36g; Carbs: 38g

Turkey And Mushroom Burgers

Preparation time: 10 minutes

Cooking time: 10 minutes

Servings: 2

Ingredients:

- 180 g mushrooms
- 500 g minced turkey
- 5 g garlic powder
- 5 g onion powder
- 2.5 g salt
- 2.5 g pepper

Directions:

1. Take your food processor, then add the mushrooms, pulsing until they form a puree. Season and pulse once more
2. Remove from the food processor and tip into a mixing bowl
3. Include turkey to the container then mix well
4. Take a small part of the mixture into your hands and shape it into burgers. You should be able to make five
5. Spray each burger with a little cooking spray and put it inside the "Air Fryer"
6. Fry at 160 °C for 10 mins

Per serving: Calories: 357.5kcal; Fat: 14g; Protein: 54g; Carbs: 0g

Chicken Breast

Preparation time: 5 minutes

Cooking time: 15 minutes

Servings: 2

Ingredients:

- Wax paper or plastic wrap
- 2 skinless/boneless chicken breast halves
- 5 g salt
- 10 g paprika
- 10 g onion powder
- 10 g black pepper
- 5 g white pepper
- 5 g cayenne pepper
- 5 g ground cumin
- 5 g ground oregano

Directions:

1. Put your chicken breasts between a few sheets of wax paper or plastic wrap and use a meat pounder until the chicken is evenly thick.

2. Make the blackened seasoning by mixing paprika, salt, onion powder, the 3 types of pepper, ground cumin, and ground oregano. Check that the spices are well mixed.
3. Dredge the chicken in the seasoning spice mixture.
4. Place the chicken breasts in the "Air Fryer" basket. Temperature to 145 °C; cook for 8 minutes.
5. After 8 minutes, remove the basket, and turn the chicken breasts over. Set the temperature to 180 °C and cook for 6 more minutes.

Per serving: Calories: 355.5kcal; Fat: 18.5g; Protein: 41.5g; Carbs: 1g

Spicy Chicken Thighs

Preparation time: 10 minutes

Cooking time: 25 minutes

Servings: 4

Ingredients:

- 80 ml low-sodium soy sauce
- Thinly sliced spring onions for garnish
- 30 ml chili garlic sauce
- Juice of 1 lime
- Toasted sesame seeds for garnish
- 2 cloves garlic, crushed
- 10 g freshly grated ginger
- 60 ml extra-virgin olive oil
- 30 ml honey
- 4 bone-in, skin-on chicken thighs

Directions:

1. Mix oil, soy sauce, honey, garlic, chili, sauce, lime juice, and ginger inside a big container. Reserve 240 ml of marinade. Add chicken thighs to the container, then toss to coat. Now cover and refrigerate for 30 minutes or more.
2. Remove 2 of the thighs from the marinade and arrange these inside the Air Fryer basket. Cook at 200 °C until thighs reach an internal temperature of 73 °C, 15-20 minutes. Now transfer the thighs to a plate and tent with foil. Now repeat with the remaining thighs.
3. Meanwhile, take a tiny pot at moderate flame, and keep the marinade to a boil. Reduce heat, and simmer until sauce thickens slightly 4-5 minutes.
4. Brush the sauce over the thighs, and garnish with spring onions and sesame seeds.

Per serving: Calories: 524kcal; Fat: 48g; Protein: 10g; Carbs: 14g

Chicken Parmesan

Preparation time: 16 minutes

Cooking time: 10 minutes

Servings: 4

Ingredients:

- 2.5 g garlic powder
- 2.5 g chili flakes
- 240 g marinara/tomato sauce
- 100 g grated mozzarella
- Freshly chopped parsley, for garnish
- 2 large boneless chicken breasts
- Salt
- 100 g panko bread crumbs
- 25 g freshly grated Parmesan
- 5 g dried oregano
- Freshly ground black pepper
- 40 g plain flour
- 2 large eggs

Directions:

1. Cut the chicken to create 4 thin pieces. Add salt and pepper on both sides.
2. Set up the skimming area by placing the wheat inside a wide, deep basin and seasoning it with a generous amount of salt and pepper. After that, crack the eggs into a separate basin and whisk together. Mix Parmesan, bread crumbs, garlic powder, oregano, and chili flakes in a third bowl.
3. One at a time, coat in flour, then dip in eggs and finally press both sides into your panko mixture.
4. Place the chicken inside the bucket of your "Air Fryer" and roast it for five mins on both ends at a temperature of 200 degrees Celsius. After topping the chicken in sauce and mozzarella, continue cooking it for a further three mins at a temperature of 200 degrees Celsius, till the cheese is melted and golden.
5. Serve with parsley garnish.

Per serving: Calories: 397kcal; Fat: 18g; Protein: 30g; Carbs: 25g

CHAPTER 9: Fruits and Vegetables

Baked Apples

Preparation time: 5 minutes

Cooking time: 5 minutes

Servings: 2

Ingredients:

- 2 green apples
- 15 g brown sugar
- 5 g ground cinnamon

Directions:

1. Preheat the air fryer to 180 °C and line the bottom of the basket with parchment paper.
2. Peel the apples and cut them into small chunks, and place them into the mesh basket. Sprinkle the sugar & cinnamon over the top and shut the air fryer lid.
3. Cook for 5 minutes until the apples have softened. Eat as a healthy and delicious snack.

Per serving: Calories: 67kcal; Fat: 1g; Protein: 1g; Carbs: 14g

Fried Bananas

Preparation time: 5 minutes

Cooking time: 5 minutes

Servings: 2

Ingredients:

- 2 medium bananas
- 15 g brown sugar
- 5 g ground nutmeg

Directions:

1. Preheat the air fryer to 180 °C and line the bottom of the basket with parchment paper.
2. Peel the bananas. Cut them in half lengthways, and place them into the lined mesh baskets. Sprinkle the top of each banana half with sugar and nutmeg.
3. Cook for five minutes until the bananas have softened and are golden and crispy.
4. Eat alongside some ice cream and a drizzle of toffee sauce.

Per serving: Calories: 97kcal; Fat: 1g; Protein: 1g; Carbs: 19g

Fried Aubergine

Preparation time: 5 minutes

Cooking time: 5 minutes

Servings: 1

Ingredients:

- 1 large aubergine
- 5 g black pepper
- 5 ml olive oil

Directions:

1. Preheat the air fryer to 200 °C and line the bottom of the basket with parchment paper.
2. Cut the aubergine in half lengthways and sprinkle with black pepper and a drizzle of olive oil.
3. Place the aubergine in the air fryer basket and cook for 5 minutes. Once cooked, remove from the air fryer and serve as a side.

Per serving: Calories: 67kcal; Fat: 3g; Protein: 2g; Carbs: 8g

Sweet Potato Fries

Preparation time: 15 minutes

Cooking time: 15 minutes

Servings: 4

Ingredients:

- 200 g sweet potato
- 15 ml olive oil

Directions:

1. Preheat the air fryer to 200 °C and line the bottom of the basket with parchment paper.
2. Cut the sweet potatoes into wedges and coat them in olive oil. Transfer to the air fryer, then cook for 12-15 minutes until crispy.
3. Serve for lunch or dinner.

Per serving: Calories: 212kcal; Fat: 6g; Protein: 6g; Carbs: 15g

Honey Roasted Carrots

Preparation time: 5 minutes

Cooking time: 5 minutes

Servings: 1

Ingredients:

- 100 g carrot sticks
- 15 ml honey

Directions:

1. Preheat the air fryer to 180 °C and line the bottom of the basket with parchment paper.
2. Coat the carrot sticks evenly in the honey and transfer them to the air fryer. Cook for 5 minutes.
3. Eat the carrot sticks as a delicious, healthy snack or side.

Per serving: Calories: 54kcal; Fat: 2g; Protein: 1g; Carbs: 4g

Crispy Air Fryer Chips

Preparation time: 5 minutes

Cooking time: 15 minutes

Servings: 4

Ingredients:

- 200 g frozen chips
- 5 g salt
- 5 ml olive oil

Directions:

1. The "air fryer" should be preheated to 200 degrees Celsius, and the lower part of the bucket should be lined using cookie sheet.
2. Put the chips inside the "air fryer" bucket and sprinkle using salt and olive oil. Fry for fifteen mins till crispy, turning halfway through.
3. Serve the chips alongside some seasoned meat or tofu.

Per serving: Calories: 265kcal; Fat: 12g; Protein: 4g; Carbs: 15g

Crispy Onion Rings

Preparation time: 15 minutes

Cooking time: 15 minutes

Servings: 8

Ingredients:

- 2 large onions
- 200 g plain flour
- 2 eggs, beaten
- 30 ml milk
- 100 g breadcrumbs
- 2.5 g onion powder
- 2.5 g garlic powder
- 5 g salt
- 5 g black pepper

Directions:

1. The "air fryer" should be preheated to 200 degrees Celsius, and the lower part of the bucket should be lined using cookie sheet.
2. Peel the onions and cut them into thick rings. Separate the rings and set them aside.
3. Get three clean bowls. In one, place the beaten eggs. In the next bowl, add the breadcrumbs. In the final bowl, place the spices, salt, and pepper.

4. Coat the onion rings first in the eggs, then the breadcrumbs, and finally in the spices. Make sure they are completely coated in breadcrumbs by the end of this step.

5. Transfer the onion rings to the lined mesh basket in the air fryer and cook for 10 minutes until golden and crispy.

6. Offer the onion rings as a side with your main meal.

Per serving: Calories: 188kcal; Fat: 8g; Protein: 5g; Carbs: 12g

Creamy Air Fryer Mash

Preparation time: 10 minutes

Cooking time: 20 minutes

Servings: 8

Ingredients:

- 2 large potatoes, peeled
- 30 g butter
- 15 ml olive oil
- 5 g black pepper
- 10 g dried chopped chives

Directions:

1. The "air fryer" should be preheated to 180 degrees Celsius, and the lower part of the bucket should be lined using cookie sheet.

2. Chop the potatoes into small chunks and add them to the air fryer basket. Cook for 20 minutes until soft.

3. Remove the potatoes from the air fryer, then use a fork or masher to mash them up into a smooth mixture.

4. Stir the butter, olive oil, black pepper, and dried chives into the mash and mix well.

5. Serve as a side with some meat, tofu, or tempeh and vegetables.

Per serving: Calories: 212kcal; Fat: 9g; Protein: 4g; Carbs: 17g

Hot and Spicy Cauliflower

Preparation time: 10 minutes

Cooking time: 10 minutes

Servings: 8

Ingredients:

- 1 head cauliflower, broken into florets
- 30 ml olive oil
- 30 ml hot sauce
- 100 g plain flour
- 5 g oregano

- 5 g smoked paprika
- 5 g chili powder
- 5 g garlic powder

Directions:

1. The "air fryer" should be preheated to 180 degrees Celsius, and the lower part of the bucket should be lined using cookie sheet.
2. Place the cauliflower florets in a bowl and drizzle the olive oil and hot sauce over the top. Toss to fully coat all of the florets.
3. In a separate bowl, combine the plain flour, oregano, smoked paprika, chili powder, and garlic powder. Stir the mixture into the cauliflower and toss to coat.
4. Transfer the cauliflower to the air fryer basket and cook for 10 minutes until hot and crispy.
5. Eat the cauliflower while hot.

Per serving: Calories: 100kcal; Fat: 4g; Protein: 3g; Carbs: 10g

Air Fryer Peppers

Preparation time: 10 minutes

Cooking time: 15 minutes

Servings: 4

Ingredients:

- 1 red bell pepper
- 15 ml olive oil

Directions:

1. The "air fryer" should be preheated to 180 degrees Celsius, and the lower part of the bucket should be lined using cookie sheet.
2. Cut the bell pepper in half and remove the seeds.   Slice the pepper into long chunks and place in the lined air fryer basket.
3. Drizzle 15 ml olive oil over the peppers, shut the air fryer lid and cook for 15 minutes until the peppers are crispy and slightly browned.
4. Serve the peppers as a side dish to your main meal.

Per serving: Calories: 41kcal; Fat: 1g; Protein: 2g; Carbs: 8g

Crispy Kale

Preparation time: 10 minutes

Cooking time: 15 minutes

Servings: 4

Ingredients:

- 100 g fresh kale
- 5 g salt

- 5 g black pepper

Directions:

1. The "air fryer" should be preheated to 200 degrees Celsius, and the lower part of the bucket should be lined using cookie sheet.
2. Chop the fresh kale into small, 1-inch chunks and sprinkle salt and black pepper through the upper part. Place in the air fryer, then cook for 15 minutes until the kale turns dry and crispy. Serve as a snack or side.

Per serving: Calories: 22kcal; Fat: 0g; Protein: 1g; Carbs: 4g

Cheese Coated Cauliflower

Preparation time: 10 minutes

Cooking time: 5 minutes

Servings: 4

Ingredients:

- 1 large cauliflower, broken into florets
- 60 g soft cheese
- 5 g black pepper
- 50 g cheddar or mozzarella cheese, grated

Directions:

1. Preheat the air fryer to 150 °C and line the mesh basket with parchment paper or lightly grease it with olive oil.
2. Wash and drain the cauliflower florets and place them in a bowl. Stir in the soft cheese and add a sprinkle of black pepper.
3. Toss to coat the cauliflower in the soft cheese and transfer to the lined air fryer basket. Top with the grated cheddar or mozzarella cheese to form an even layer over the cauliflower.
4. Close the lid of the air fryer, then cook the cauliflower for 5 minutes until it has softened and the cheese has melted on top. If you prefer the cheese to be crispy, cook for a few more minutes to bake the cheese.
5. Serve the cheesy cauliflower as a side dish with your dinner.

Per serving: Calories: 87kcal; Fat: 4g; Protein: 3g; Carbs: 3g

Tomato Quorn Fillets

Preparation time: 5 minutes

Cooking time: 15 minutes

Servings: 4

Ingredients:

- 4 pcs - 100 g Quorn fillets
- 60 g tomato puree

- 15 g dried mixed herbs

Directions:

1. The "air fryer" should be preheated to 180 degrees Celsius, and the lower part of the bucket should be lined using cookie sheet.

2. Lay the Quorn fillets out on a clean surface.

3. In a bowl, mix the tomato puree and dried mixed herbs. Spread the tomato mixture over the Quorn fillets and transfer to the air fryer. Cook for 12-15 minutes until golden and hot.

4. Serve the fillets with a side of chips and vegetables or chop them up to stir into a pasta dish.

Per serving: Calories: 201kcal; Fat: 5g; Protein: 14g; Carbs: 8g

CHAPTER 10: Side Dish

Garlic Cauliflower

Preparation time: 10 minutes

Cooking time: 15 minutes

Servings: 2-3

Ingredients:

- 30 g ghee or butter, melted
- Freshly ground black pepper
- 2.5 g garlic powder
- 1.25 g turmeric
- Salt
- 1 small head of cauliflower cut into small florets

Directions:

1. Take a small bowl and whisk turmeric, ghee, and garlic powder. Place cauliflower in a large bowl, pour over the ghee mixture and toss to coat until all the florets are yellow. Add a good amount of salt & pepper.
2. Preheat your Air Fryer to 190 °C for 3 minutes. Arrange the cauliflower in a single layer into the basket and cook, toss halfway through, until golden brown, 10-12 minutes.

Per serving: Calories: 114.5kcal; Fat: 11.5g; Protein: 1g; Carbs: 2.5g

Air Fryer Burritos

Preparation time: 5 minutes

Cooking time: 5 minutes

Servings: 4

Ingredients:

- 4 tortilla wraps
- 120 g cooked white rice
- 60 g mozzarella cheese, grated
- 1 pc - 400 g can black beans, drained & rinsed
- 1 pc - 400 g can chopped tomatoes
- ½ onion, finely sliced
- 15 ml lime juice
- 15 g salsa

Directions:

1. Preheat the air fryer to 190 °C and line the bottom of the basket with parchment paper.

2. Lay out the tortilla wraps and spoon 30 g of cooked white rice into the center of each one alongside 15 g of mozzarella cheese.

3. In a mixing bowl, combine black beans, chopped tomatoes, and sliced onions. Squeeze in a touch of lime juice & salsa.

4. Evenly spoon the mixture on top of the rice and cheese in the center of each wrap.

5. Carefully roll the wraps up into burritos and use a cocktail stick to keep them tightly rolled up. Place them into the lined air fryer basket and cook for 5-7 minutes until hot and slightly crispy.

Per serving: Calories: 312kcal; Fat: 11g; Protein: 16g; Carbs: 21g

Fried Chips

Preparation time: 5 minutes

Cooking time: 20 minutes

Servings: 4

Ingredients:

- Salt
- 1 kg of potatoes, peeled, cut into 1cm batons
- Oil spray (vegetable or sunflower works best)
- Other optional seasonings
- Your favorite dip

Directions:

1. Preheat to 180 °C. Rinse the chips in cold water, then pat them dry.

2. Place the chips into the Air Fryer basket and spray with oil. Sprinkle them with salt & any other seasoning you want, then shake the basket.

3. Air fry for 20 minutes, and shake the chips halfway through to ensure even cooking. After it finishes, if the chips are not well cooked, place them back inside for 5 minutes more and continue to do so until they are good to go.

4. Serve with your favorite dip.

Per serving: Calories: 192.5kcal; Fat: 0g; Protein: 5g; Carbs: 43.5g

Broccoli with Oil

Preparation time: 5 minutes

Cooking time: 10 minutes

Servings: 4

Ingredients:

- 1 medium head broccoli, cut into florets
- 15 ml extra-virgin olive oil
- 1 clove garlic, crushed
- Salt

- Freshly ground black pepper
- Pinch chili flakes

Directions:

1. Take a large bowl, and toss broccoli with garlic and oil. Season with salt, pepper, and chili flakes.
2. Arrange the broccoli in a single layer inside the basket. Cook for 10 minutes at 180 °C, until tender and crisp. Repeat with the remaining part.

Per serving: Calories: 81kcal; Fat: 4g; Protein: 4g; Carbs: 10g

3-Bean Chili Mix

Preparation time: 5 minutes

Cooking time: 20 minutes

Servings: 4

Ingredients:

- 1 pc - 400 g can kidney beans, drained & rinsed
- 1 pc - 400 g can white beans, drained & rinsed
- 1 pc - 400 g can chopped tomatoes
- 15 ml olive oil
- 5 g dried mixed herbs
- 5 g chili powder

Directions:

1. Preheat the air fryer to 180 °C and line the bottom of the basket with parchment paper.
2. In a large mixing bowl, combine the kidney beans, white beans, chopped tomatoes, olive oil, dried mixed herbs, and chili powder. Stir until fully combined.
3. Transfer to the air fryer basket, then cook for 25-30 minutes until the mixture is hot and the beans have softened.
4. Serve the chili with some fresh yogurt and rice.

Per serving: Calories: 212kcal; Fat: 7g; Protein: 13g; Carbs: 17g

Courgette Sticks

Preparation time: 10 minutes

Cooking time: 20 minutes

Servings: 4

Ingredients:

- 2 medium courgette sliced into 1/2cm rounds
- 2 large eggs
- 90 g panko bread crumbs
- 50 g cornmeal

- 35 g freshly grated 182
- 5 g dried oregano
- 1.125 g garlic powder
- Pinch chili flakes
- Salt
- Freshly ground black pepper
- Marinara, for serving

Directions:

1. Arrange the courgette on a platter lined with paper towels and pat dry.
2. Arrange the beaten eggs in a shallow bowl. Take another shallow bowl, and mix cornmeal, panko, oregano, Parmesan, garlic powder, and a large pinch of chili flakes. Add salt and pepper.
3. One at a time, dip the courgette rounds into the egg, then into the panko mixture, and press to coat.
4. Arrange the courgette in an even layer, cook at 200 °C for 18 minutes, and flip halfway through.
5. Serve warm with marinara.

Per serving: Calories: 182kcal; Fat: 5g; Protein: 6.6g; Carbs: 22g

Fried Bacon

Preparation time: 10 minutes

Cooking time: 10 minutes

Servings: 2

Ingredients:

- 4-5 rashers of lean bacon, fat cut off

Directions:

1. Line up the Air Fryer basket with parchment paper to soak up excess grease.
2. Arrange your bacon in the basket, ensuring you don't overcrowd; around 4-5 slices should be enough, depending upon the size of your machine.
3. Set the fryer to 200 °C.
4. Cook for 10 minutes for crispy, and an extra 2 if you want it super-crispy.
5. Serve and enjoy!

Per serving: Calories: 161kcal; Fat: 12g; Protein: 12g; Carbs: 0.5g

Patatas Bravas

Preparation time: 10 minutes

Cooking time: 25 minutes

Servings: 4

Ingredients:

- 300g potatoes, cut into chunks

- 15 ml avocado oil
- 5 g garlic powder
- Pinch of salt
- Pinch of pepper
- 15 g smoked paprika

Directions:

1. Take a large saucepan of water and bring to boil; add potatoes, cooking for 6 minutes.
2. Strain your potatoes, place them on a piece of kitchen towel, and once a little cool, pat dry.
3. Leave the potatoes to arrive at room temperate.
4. Take a huge mixing bowl, then add the garlic powder, salt, and pepper and add the avocado oil, mixing.
5. Add now your potatoes to the bowl and coat liberally.
6. Place the potatoes into the basket and arrange them with space in between.
7. Set your fryer to 200 °C.
8. Cook the potatoes for 15 minutes, giving them a shake at the halfway point.
9. Remove and serve.

Per serving: Calories: 88.5kcal; Fat: 3.5g; Protein: 1.5g; Carbs: 13g

Bacon Muffins

Preparation time: 7 minutes

Cooking time: 6 minutes

Servings: 1

Ingredients:

- 1 Large Egg
- 1 Slice of Unsmoked Bacon
- 1 English All Butter Muffin
- 2 Slices of Burger Cheese
- 1 Pinch of Salt and Pepper

Directions:

1. Crack the large egg into either a ramekin or oven-proof dish.
2. Slice the muffin in half.
3. Layer 1 slice of burger cheese on 1 half.
4. Place now the muffin and bacon in the Air Fryer drawer, and place the ovenproof dish or ramekin in the drawer too.
5. Heat up the Air Fryer to 200 °C for 6 minutes.
6. Once it is done, assemble the breakfast muffin and add the extra slice of cheese on top.

Per serving: Calories: 291kcal; Fat: 12g; Protein: 15g; Carbs: 25g

Crispy Air Fryer Falafel

Preparation time: 10 minutes

Cooking time: 15 minutes

Servings: 4

Ingredients:

- ½ onion, sliced
- 2 cloves garlic, peeled and sliced
- 30 g fresh parsley leaves, finely chopped
- 30 g fresh coriander leaves, finely chopped
- 2 pcs - 400 g chickpeas, drained and rinsed
- 5 g dried mixed herbs
- 5 g smoked paprika
- 5 g salt
- 5 g black pepper
- 5 g baking powder

Directions:

1. Preheat the air fryer to 180 °C and line the bottom of the basket with parchment paper.
2. Add the onion, garlic cloves, fresh parsley, and fresh coriander to a food processor and pulse in 30-second intervals until all ingredients are fully combined. Scrape the mixture off the sides of the food processor in between intervals if necessary.
3. Add the chickpeas, dried mixed herbs, smoked paprika, salt, black pepper, and baking powder. Pulse the mixture until fully combined. Add more water if necessary. The mixture should be dry but not too crumbly, and it should be easy to form into balls.
4. Use a spoon to scoop about 30 g of the mixture at a time and roll it into small balls. Place the falafel balls into the lined air fryer basket.
5. Cook the falafel balls for 12-15 minutes until golden and crispy on the edges.
6. Serve the falafels hot or cold with some hummus or tahini sauce. Alternatively, add them to some wholemeal pitta bread or a wrap.

Per serving: Calories: 188kcal; Fat: 6g; Protein: 9g; Carbs: 13g

Roast Potatoes

Preparation time: 30 minutes

Cooking time: 30-60 minutes

Servings: 2

Ingredients:

- 2 large floury potatoes (approximately 450g)
- Salt, to taste

- 15 ml olive oil

Directions:

1. Peel, and quarter your potatoes, then boil them in a saucepan of salted water for 15 minutes (place them when the water is already boiling).
2. Now drain the potatoes, and leave them to steam dry for a minute or two.
3. Toss with olive oil & a good amount of salt.
4. Air fry for 30 minutes, 200 °C, and toss every 10 minutes.
5. Serve.

Per serving: Calories: 232.5kcal; Fat: 7g; Protein: 4.5g; Carbs: 39g

Crispy Smoked Paprika Chickpeas

Preparation time: 5 minutes

Cooking time: 10 minutes

Servings: 4

Ingredients:

- 1 pc - 400 g can chickpeas, drained & rinsed
- 15 ml olive oil
- 15 g smoked paprika
- 5 g cayenne pepper

Directions:

1. Preheat the air fryer to 190 °C and line the bottom of the basket with parchment paper.
2. Place the chickpeas in a bowl and sprinkle over the smoked paprika, cayenne pepper, and olive oil. Toss to fully coat the chickpeas.
3. Transfer the chickpeas to the air fryer, then cook for 10-12 minutes until they're crispy and golden.
4. Serve the chickpeas as a side or snack.

Per serving: Calories: 129kcal; Fat: 6g; Protein: 14g; Carbs: 18g

Aubergine

Preparation time: 9 minutes

Cooking time: 15 minutes

Servings: 4

Ingredients:

- 1 medium aubergine
- 15 ml extra-virgin olive oil
- 5 g dried oregano
- 2.5 g garlic powder
- Salt

- Freshly ground black pepper
- Pinch chili flakes

Directions:

1. Take the aubergine and cut the ends off, then cut it in half (lengthwise). Now cut each half into strips about 2.5 cm thick and 7 cm long. Take a medium bowl, add oil, aubergine, and seasonings, and toss to coat.
2. Arrange a single layer into the Air Fryer basket. Cook 190 °C for 14 minutes until golden. Shake the basket once about halfway through.

Per serving: Calories: 58kcal; Fat: 3.5g; Protein: 1g; Carbs: 6.5g

Green Beans

Preparation time: 2 minutes

Cooking time: 7 minutes

Servings: 2

Ingredients:

- 5 ml of lemon juice
- 2.5 g of Garlic Powder
- 320 g of Fresh Green Beans
- 5 ml of Olive oil
- 2.5 g of Salt
- 2.5 g of Ground Pepper
- 2.5 g of Italian Seasoning

Optional Garnish:

- Lemon Wedge
- Herbs- Parsley Thyme
- Chilli Flakes

Directions:

1. Trim the beans.
2. Prepare a seasoning mixture with all the ingredients except the beans.
3. Now pour the mixture on the beans, and toss to coat well.
4. Preheat your Air Fryer to 200 °C for 2 minutes.
5. Arrange the beans inside.
6. Air fry for 7-8 minutes, 200 °C.
7. Serve with optional garnish.

Per serving: Calories: 50.5kcal; Fat: 0.5g; Protein: 2.5g; Carbs: 10g

CHAPTER 11: Snacks and Desserts

Chocolate Bark

Preparation time: 10 minutes

Cooking time: 5 minutes

Servings: 8

Ingredients:

- 10 squares of milk chocolate, melted
- 15 g chopped nuts
- 15 g mixed dried fruit (raisins, sultanas, dried apricots)

Directions:

1. Preheat the air fryer to 180 °C.
2. Remove the mesh basket from the air fryer and line the bottom with parchment paper.
3. In a bowl, mix the melted chocolate, chopped nuts, and dried fruit. Pour into the lined mesh basket.
4. Transfer the mesh basket to the air fryer and cook for 3 to 5 minutes. Remove the chocolate from the air fryer and leave two sets in the freezer.

Per serving: Calories: 112kcal; Fat: 6g; Protein: 3g; Carbs: 12g

Easy Banana Protein Pancakes

Preparation time: 5 minutes

Cooking time: 20 minutes

Servings: 2

Ingredients:

- 2 bananas
- 2 eggs, beaten
- 128 g vanilla protein powder

Directions:

1. Preheat the air fryer to 180 °C and line the bottom of the basket with parchment paper.
2. Peel the bananas and mash them in a bowl using a fork.
3. Whisk the eggs into the bowl and pour half of the batter into the lined air fryer basket.
4. Allow the batter to spread into a pancake shape across the bottom of the machine and cook for 10 minutes until golden and crispy.
5. Carefully remove the pancake and set it aside while you cook the other pancake. Put the remaining half of the batter into the air fryer while it's still hot and cook for 10 minutes.
6. Serve the two pancakes with some fresh fruit and honey.

Per serving: Calories: 110kcal; Fat: 3g; Protein: 10g; Carbs: 10g

Chocolate and Blueberry Pop Tarts

Preparation time: 15 minutes

Cooking time: 10 minutes

Servings: 8

Ingredients:

For the filling:

- 50 g fresh blueberries
- 50 g chocolate chips
- 100 g granulated sugar
- 50 g granulated sugar
- 5 g corn starch

For the pastry:

- 1 sheet puff pastry

For the frosting:

- 60 g powdered sugar
- 15 ml maple syrup

Directions:

1. Preheat the air fryer to 180 °C and line the mesh basket with parchment paper or grease it with olive oil.
2. Make the filling by combining the blueberries, chocolate chips, granulated sugar, and brown sugar in a saucepan over medium heat. Stir until the mixture starts to boil before lowering the temperature. Heat through until it forms a smooth, consistent mixture.
3. Whisk in the corn starch and simmer for 2 minutes. Remove the saucepan from the heat and set aside to cool.
4. Meanwhile, prepare the pastry. Roll out the large sheet of puff pastry and cut it into 8 equal rectangles.
5. Spoon 30 g of the cooled blueberry and chocolate filling onto one side of each rectangle. Fold over the other side of each puff pastry rectangle to cover the filling. Press the sides down with a fork or use your fingers to seal the filling into the pastry.
6. Carefully place puff pastry rectangles into the prepared air fryer basket and cook for 10-12 minutes 'til the pastry is golden and crispy on all sides.
7. While the puff pastry pop tarts are cooking, make the frosting by combining the powdered sugar and maple syrup in a bowl.
8. When the puff pastry sheets are cool, spread a layer of frosting on one side of each pop tart. Allow the frosting to set before serving.
9. Store the leftover pop tarts in the fridge.

Per serving: Calories: 232kcal; Fat: 13g; Protein: 5g; Carbs: 28g

Vanilla Cheesecake

Preparation time: 1 hour 10 minutes

Cooking time: none

Servings: 8

Ingredients:

For the base:

- 200 g cracker or digestive biscuits
- 60 g butter, melted
- 30 g brown sugar

For the cheesecake:

- 400 g cream cheese
- 200 g granulated sugar
- 30 g plain flour
- 60 g sour cream
- 5 g vanilla extract
- 2 eggs, beaten

Directions:

1. Preheat the air fryer to 150 °C, then line a loaf tin with greaseproof paper.
2. In a bowl, combine the crackers or biscuits, melted butter, and brown sugar. Mix until the cracker or biscuit crumbs are moist
3. Transfer the crumbs to the prepared loaf tin and lightly press into the bottom to form an even base.
4. Bake the crust in the air fryer for 10 minutes.
5. Remove the crust from the air fryer, then set it aside to cool while you prepare the filling. Leave the air fryer running at the same temperature setting.
6. In a huge mixing bowl, whisk together the cream cheese, granulated sugar, plain flour, sour cream, and vanilla extract until they form a smooth mixture.
7. Fold in the eggs, one at a time.
8. Spoon the wet mixture onto the top of the baked crust. Use the back of a spoon or spatula to even out the top of the cheesecake.
9. Transfer the cheesecake back to the air fryer and cook for 20 minutes.
10. Remove the cheesecake from the air fryer and store it in the fridge overnight to set. Serve cold with a side of ice cream or whipped cream.

Per serving: Calories: 364kcal; Fat: 14g; Protein: 7g; Carbs: 18g

Scrambled Tofu With Soy Sauce

Preparation time: 5 minutes

Cooking time: 10 minutes

Servings: 4

Ingredients:

- 1 pc - 400 g block firm tofu
- 30 ml soy sauce
- 5 g black pepper

Directions:

1. Preheat the air fryer to 200 °C and line the bottom of the basket with parchment paper.
2. Cut the tofu into even chunks and place the soy sauce in a small bowl. Toss the tofu pieces to coat in the sauce. Sprinkle some black pepper over the tofu and transfer to the air fryer.
3. Cook the tofu for 10 minutes until crispy on the edges. Once cooked, remove the tofu and use a fork to scramble.
4. Serve for lunch while hot. You can eat the scrambled tofu on toast or stir in some vegetables for a larger meal.

Per serving: Calories: 198kcal; Fat: 10g; Protein: 12g; Carbs: 12g

Sweet and Sticky Tofu

Preparation time: 15 minutes

Cooking time: 15 minutes

Servings: 4

Ingredients:

- 5 g onion powder
- 5 g garlic powder
- 45 ml soy sauce
- 45 ml sweet chili sauce
- 5 ml hot sauce
- 1 pc - 400 g block firm tofu, cubed
- 45 g corn starch

Directions:

1. Preheat your air fryer to 180 °C and line the bottom of the basket with parchment paper.
2. In a mixing bowl, combine the onion powder, garlic powder, soy sauce, sweet chili sauce, and hot sauce.
3. Toss the tofu cubes in the sauce until fully coated. Refrigerate for 20 minutes to marinate.
4. Place the corn starch in a separate bowl and coat the tofu. Transfer the tofu to the lined air fryer basket. Cook for 15 minutes until hot and crispy.
5. Serve the tofu while hot with some pasta or noodles and veggies.

Per serving: Calories: 301kcal; Fat: 7g; Protein: 15g; Carbs: 9g

Crispy BBQ Tempeh

Preparation time: 5 minutes

Cooking time: 10 minutes

Servings: 4

Ingredients:

- 1 pc - 400 g block tempeh
- 30 ml BBQ sauce

Directions:

1. Preheat the air fryer to 200 °C and line the bottom of the basket with parchment paper.
2. Cut the tempeh into even chunks and coat in BBQ sauce. Transfer into the air fryer basket and cook for 10 minutes until the tempeh is sticky and crispy.
3. Serve the tempeh with some fresh noodles or brown rice and vegetables.

Per serving: Calories: 198kcal; Fat: 10g; Protein: 12g; Carbs: 12g

Tomato and Herb Tofu

Preparation time: 5 minutes

Cooking time: 10 minutes

Servings: 4

Ingredients:

- 1 pc - 400 g block extra firm tofu
- 30 g tomato and herb pasta sauce
- 5 g black pepper

Directions:

1. Preheat the air fryer to 200 °C and line the bottom of the basket with parchment paper.
2. Cut the tofu into even chunks.
3. Mix the tomato and herb sauce and the black pepper in a bowl. Coat the tofu piece in the sauce and place it in the lined air fryer basket.
4. Cook the tofu for 12-15 minutes until crispy on the edges. Serve the tofu in a stir fry or pasta dish or add it to your salad.

Per serving: Calories: 198kcal; Fat: 10g; Protein: 12g; Carbs: 12g

British Victoria Sponge

Preparation time: 15 minutes

Cooking time: 28 minutes

Servings: 8

Ingredients:

For the Victoria Sponge:

- 100 g Plain Flour
- 100 g Butter
- 100 g Caster Sugar
- 2 Medium Eggs

For the Cake Filling:

- 30 g Strawberry Jam
- 50 g Butter
- 100 g Icing Sugar
- 15 g Whipped Cream

Directions:

1. Preheat the Air Fryer to 180 °C.
2. Grease a baking dish.
3. Cream the sugar and the butter until light and fluffy.
4. Now beat in the eggs, and add a little flour with each.
5. Now gently fold in the flour.
6. Arrange your mixture into the tin and cook for 15 minutes, 180 °C, then 10 minutes, 170 °C.
7. Now leave it to cool and once it is cooled, slice into two equal slices of sponge.
8. Now make the filling: Cream the butter until you have a thick creamy mixture; gradually add icing sugar and whipped cream.
9. Arrange a layer of strawberry jam, then a layer of cake filling, and add your other sponge on top.
10. Serve!

Per serving: Calories: 243kcal; Fat: 16.5g; Protein: 3g; Carbs: 21g

Lemon Biscuits

Preparation time: 5 minutes

Cooking time: 5 minutes

Servings: 9

Ingredients:

- 100 g Butter
- 100 g Caster Sugar
- 225 g Self-Raising Flour
- 1 Small Lemon (rind and juice)
- 1 Small Egg
- 5 g Vanilla Essence

Directions:

1. Preheat the Air Fryer to 180 °C.

2. Mix flour and sugar in a bowl. Add the butter, then rub it in until your mix resembles breadcrumbs. Shake your bowl regularly so that the fat bits come to the top so that you know what you have left to rub in.

3. Add the lemon rind and juice along with the egg.

4. Combine and knead until you have a lovely soft dough.

5. Roll out and cut into medium-sized biscuits.

6. Place the biscuits into the Air Fryer on a baking sheet and cook for five minutes at 180 °C.

7. Place on a cooling tray and sprinkle with icing sugar.

Per serving: Calories: 205kcal; Fat: 10g; Protein: 3.5g; Carbs: 26g

Soft Chocolate Brownies

Preparation time: 20 minutes

Cooking time: 18 minutes

Servings: 10

Ingredients:

- 125 g Caster Sugar
- 30 ml Water
- 142 ml Milk
- 125 g Butter
- 50 g Chocolate
- 175 g Brown Sugar
- 2 Medium Eggs (beaten)
- 100 g Self Raising Flour
- 10 g Vanilla Essence

Directions:

1. Preheat your Air Fryer to 180 °C.

2. Prepare the chocolate brownies: Melt 100 g of butter and the chocolate in a bowl above a pan over medium heat. Stir in the brown sugar, now add the eggs and then add the vanilla essence. Add the self-raising flour and mix well.

3. Pour the mixture into a greased dish that is of an appropriate size for your Air Fryer.

4. Cook into the Air Fryer for 15 minutes, 180 °C.

5. While the brownies are cooking, it is time to make the caramel sauce – Mix the caster sugar & the water in a pan on medium heat until the sugar is melted. Then turn it up and cook for another 3 minutes until it has turned a light brown color. Take off the heat and then after 2 minutes, add your butter and keep stirring until it is all melted. Then slowly add the milk.

6. Set the caramel sauce to one side for it to cool.

7. When the brownies are ready, chop them into squares, place them on a plate with some sliced bananas, and cover them with caramel sauce.

8. Serve!

Per serving: Calories: 249kcal; Fat: 13g; Protein: 3.5g; Carbs: 30g

Fruit Crumble

Preparation time: 15 minutes

Cooking time: 15 minutes

Servings: 6

Ingredients:

- 75 g Plain Flour
- 33 g Butter
- 30 g Caster Sugar
- 1 Medium Red Apple1
- 4 Medium Plums
- 50 g Frozen Berries
- 5 g Cinnamon

Directions:

1. Preheat your Air Fryer to 180 °C.
2. Take a suitable dish that will fit in your Air Fryer, then add the fruit. Peel and dice everything, and check it is all of a similar size.
3. Place plain flour in a mixing bowl along with sugar and mix in the butter. Rub the fat into the flour until your mixture resembles breadcrumbs.
4. Arrange your crumble mixture over the fruit and place it into the Air Fryer.
5. Cook 15 minutes, 180 °C.
6. Serve!

Per serving: Calories: 141kcal; Fat: 4.5g; Protein: 1.6g; Carbs: 24g

Mini Apple Pie

Preparation time: 5 minutes

Cooking time: 18 minutes

Servings: 9

Ingredients:

- 75 g Plain Flour
- 33 g Butter
- 15 g Caster Sugar
- Water
- 2 Medium Red Apples
- Pinch Cinnamon

- Pinch Caster Sugar

Directions:

1. Preheat your Air Fryer to 180 °C.
2. Start by making your pastry – place the plain flour and butter in a mixing bowl and rub the fat into the flour. Add the sugar and mix well. Add the water until the ingredients are moist enough to combine into a nice dough. Knead the dough well until it has a smooth texture.
3. Cover your pastry tins with butter to stop them from sticking, and then roll out the pastry and fill your pastry tins.
4. Peel, dice your apples, and place them in the tins. Sprinkle them with sugar and cinnamon.
5. Add an extra pastry layer to the top and make some fork markings so that they can breathe.
6. Cook in the Air Fryer for 18 mins.

Per serving: Calories: 85kcal; Fat: 3g; Protein: 1g; Carbs: 13.5g

Shortbread Chocolate Balls

Preparation time: 4 minutes

Cooking time: 13 minutes

Servings: 9

Ingredients:

- 175 g Butter
- 75 g Caster Sugar
- 250 g Plain Flour
- 5 g Vanilla Essence
- 9 Chocolate chunks
- 30 g Cocoa

Directions:

1. Preheat your Air Fryer to 180 °C.
2. Take a bowl and mix your sugar, flour, and cocoa.
3. Rub in the butter, and knead well until you see a smooth dough.
4. Now divide into balls, place a chunk of chocolate into the center of each one, and make sure none of the chocolate chunks is showing.
5. Place your chocolate shortbread balls onto a baking sheet in your Air Fryer. Cook them at 180 °C for 8 minutes and then another 5 minutes at 160 °C so that you can make sure they are cooked in the middle.
6. Serve!

Per serving: Calories: 297kcal; Fat: 18g; Protein: 4g; Carbs: 31g

Strawberry Cupcakes

Preparation time: 15 minutes

Cooking time: 8 minutes

Servings: 10

Ingredients:

- 100 g Butter
- 100 g Caster Sugar
- 2 Medium Eggs
- 100 g Self Raising Flour
- 2.5 g Vanilla Essence
- 50 g Butter
- 100 g Icing Sugar
- 2.5 g Pink Food Colouring
- 15 g Whipped Cream
- 40 g Fresh Strawberries (blended)

Directions:

1. Preheat the Air Fryer to 170 °C.
2. Meanwhile, cream the sugar and butter using a large mixing bowl. Do this until your mixture is light and fluffy.
3. Add the vanilla essence and beat in the eggs one at a time. After adding each egg add a little of the flour. Gently fold in the remaining flour.
4. Add them to little bun cases so that they are 80% full.
5. Place them in the Air Fryer and then cook for 8 minutes at 170 °C.
6. Meanwhile, make the topping: Cream the butter and gradually add the icing sugar until you have a creamy mixture. Add the food coloring, whipped cream, and blended strawberries, and mix well.
7. Once the cupcakes are cooked, using a piping bag, add your topping to them, making circular motions so that you have that lovely cupcake look.
8. Serve!

Per serving: Calories: 231kcal; Fat: 13g; Protein: 2.5g; Carbs: 26g

CHAPTER 12: Measurement Conversion Chart

Volume Equivalents (Liquid)

US Standard	US Standard (ounces)	Metric (approximate)
2 tablespoons	1 fl. oz.	30 mL
¼ cup	2 fl. oz.	60 mL
½ cup	4 fl. oz.	120 mL
1 cup	8 fl. oz.	240 mL
1½ cups	12 fl. oz.	355 mL
2 cups or 1 pint	16 fl. oz.	475 mL
4 cups or 1 quart	32 fl. oz.	1 L
1 gallon	128 fl. oz.	4 L

Volume Equivalents (Dry)

US Standard	Metric (approximate)
⅛ teaspoon	0.5 mL
¼ teaspoon	1 mL
½ teaspoon	2 mL
¾ teaspoon	4 mL
1 teaspoon	5 mL
1 tablespoon	15 mL
¼ cup	59 mL
⅓ cup	79 mL
½ cup	118 mL
⅔ cup	156 mL
¾ cup	177 mL
1 cup	235 mL
2 cups or 1 pint	475 mL
3 cups	700 mL
4 cups or 1 quart	1 L

Oven Temperatures

Fahrenheit (F)	Celsius (C) (approximate)
250°F	120°C
300°F	150°C
325°F	165°C
350°F	180°C

375°F	190°C
400°F	200°C
425°F	220°C
450°F	230°C

Weight Equivalents

US Standard	Metric (approximate)
1 tablespoon	15 g
½ ounce	15 g
1 ounce	30 g
2 ounces	60 g
4 ounces	115 g
8 ounces	225 g
12 ounces	340 g
16 ounces or 1 pound	455 g

CHAPTER 13: 30-Day Meal Plan

Days	Breakfast	Lunch	Dinner	Dessert
1	Breakfast Toasties	Beef Fried Rice	Chicken Bites	Vanilla Cheesecake
2	Air Fryer Naan Bread Pizzas	Breaded Cod Fillets	Mozzarella-Stuffed Meatballs	Fried Chips
3	Chocolate Chip Cookies	Tomato And Herb Chicken Breast	Pork Chops	Soft Chocolate Brownies
4	Sausage Sandwiches	Spicy Chicken Thighs	Coconut Prawns	Bacon Muffins
5	French Toast Sticks	Lamb Steaks	Rotisserie Chicken	Shortbread Chocolate Balls
6	Sweet Potato Hash	Tuna Patties	Fried Cod	Fried Bacon
7	Egg Fried Rice	Turkey And Mushroom Burgers	Beef Wellington	Crispy Bbq Tempeh
8	BBQ Chicken Toasted Wraps	Chicken Satay	Sriracha With Salmon	Broccoli With Oil
9	Cinnamon French Toast	Roast Pork	Chicken Parmesan	British Victoria Sponge
10	Cinnamon Bagels	Herby Breaded Fish	Breaded Cod Fillets	Green Beans
11	Cheese Omelette	Chicken Wings With Honey And Sesame	Air Fryer Pigs In Blankets	Easy Banana Protein Pancakes
12	Crispy Pizza Bites	Mozzarella-Stuffed Meatballs	Peppery Lemon Shrimp	Roast Potatoes
13	Air Fryer Garlic Bread	Mozzarella-Stuffed Meatballs	Air Fryer Turkey Breast	Sweet And Sticky Tofu
14	Vegetable Frittata	Baked Crunchy Cod	Tuna Patties	Patatas Bravas
15	Egg & Ham Cups	Chicken Wings	Mustard Glazed Pork	Chocolate Bark
16	Vegetable Rice	Chicken Wings With Honey And Sesame	Air Fryer Tuna Steak	Courgette Sticks
17	Egg Fried Rice	Cheesy Beef Enchiladas	Turkey Burgers	Chocolate And Blueberry Pop Tarts
18	BBQ Chicken Toasted Wraps	Tilapia Fillets	Roast Pork	Garlic Cauliflower

19	Cinnamon French Toast	Chicken Nuggets	Simple Hamburgers	Mini Apple Pie
20	Cinnamon Bagels	Peppery Lemon Shrimp	Simple Salmon	Crispy Air Fryer Falafel
21	Breakfast Toasties	Beef Meatballs	Spicy Chicken Thighs	Tomato And Herb Tofu
22	Air Fryer Naan Bread Pizzas	Fish Tacos	Spicy Chicken Thighs	Crispy Smoked Paprika Chickpeas
23	Chocolate Chip Cookies	Chicken Tenders	Grilled Sausages	Scrambled Tofu With Soy Sauce
24	Sausage Sandwiches	Cheesy Beef Enchiladas	Crab Cakes	Aubergine
25	French Toast Sticks	Beef Kebobs	Chicken Strips	Strawberry Cupcakes
26	Sweet Potato Hash	Fried Cod	Mustard Glazed Pork	Air Fryer Burritos
27	Cheese Omelette	Chicken Breast	Herbed Steak	Lemon Biscuits
28	Crispy Pizza Bites	Rotisserie Chicken	Chicken Satay	Baked Apples
29	Air Fryer Garlic Bread	Beef Fried Rice	Chicken Bites	Fruit Crumble
30	Vegetable Frittata	Breaded Cod Fillets	Mozzarella-Stuffed Meatballs	Fried Bananas

CHAPTER 14: Conclusion

Many people use an air fryer to help them lose weight, which is possible because it is so easy to use. Most air fryers don't make a big mess, so you don't have to worry about the frying oil ruining your kitchen or getting all over your clothes. They also seem less dangerous than deep frying in the oven, stovetop, microwave, or even skillet. Compared with other cooking methods that may take longer periods, the cook times can be greatly reduced.

The air fryer is not just good for the home cook. It can also be a great addition to your kitchen if you own a business. Not only will it help you make some extra bucks, but it will also help attract more customers as well. There are plenty of things that you can make at home with an air fryer. You can easily cook up homemade fries, onion rings, chicken wings, and many other foods with this machine.

These tools have become much more popular over the last couple of years, and people are still finding new recipes to try out. Some places specialize in selling these machines because so many people see the benefits they offer when used correctly. It can be hard to find the time to go out and buy a new piece of kitchen equipment like this, so people usually look for something that is easy to use and doesn't take up a lot of room. If you want to get an air fryer, then it is important to learn more about them online first.

There are a lot of tutorials that you can find on the web, but it is best if you just get one from a professional. You may need some help at first getting used to how the machine works and what kind of foods work with it best. If you see all the different recipes that people have tried with this tool, you will probably feel inspired to proceed with yours.

While it is becoming more common to find an air fryer in kitchens all over the world, there are still some people that don't know much about them or have never used one before. You will have to choose the best model for your needs and your budget, so make sure you take some time to compare different brands.

There are plenty of good air fryer reviews online that you can read before buying one of these tools. It is also important that you read all of the instructions carefully before you start cooking with it. As long as this machine is cleaned and maintained in a proper manner then it should last for a long time as well.

CHAPTER 15: Index

Simple Salmon; 36
Soft Chocolate Brownies; 76
Spicy Chicken Thighs; 53
Sriracha With Salmon; 41
Strawberry Cupcakes; 78
Sweet and Sticky Tofu; 73
Sweet Potato Fries; 56
Sweet Potato Hash; 21
Tilapia Fillets; 38

Tomato and Herb Chicken Breast; 47
Tomato and Herb Tofu; 74
Tomato Quorn Fillets; 60
Tuna Patties; 40
Turkey And Mushroom Burgers; 51
Turkey Burgers; 45
Vanilla Cheesecake; 72
Vegetable Frittata; 22
Vegetable Rice; 18

Printed in Great Britain
by Amazon

16405770R00050